God Is My Father

NICK CUTHBERT

KINGSWAY PUBLICATIONS
EASTBOURNE

First published 1986

ISBN 0 86065 363 3

Front cover photo: Barbara Kieve, The Image Bank

Printed in Great Britain for
KINGSWAY PUBLICATIONS LTD
Lottbridge Drove, Eastbourne, E. Sussex BN23 6NT by
Cox & Wyman Ltd, Reading.
Typeset by Nuprint Services Ltd, Harpenden, Herts AL5 4SE.

To Lois

Contents

Acknowledgements

This book was finished some time ago but its completion coincided with the publication of Floyd McClung's excellent book *The Father Heart of God*. It was significant that we had both independently been working on the same theme—and with the same working title. Although we've approached this subject from different angles I believe it underlines the importance of the message at this time of great uncertainty.

I want to express thanks to Andrew and Mark who are not only my sons but who have become my friends. They have been the means of teaching me so much about fatherhood. I'm indebted also to Kate Hayes and Kerrie Jones for all their hard work in typing and re-typing, and also to the fellowship of friends here in the Moseley and Kings Heath area of Birmingham. It is impossible to adequately express how much I owe to my wife Lois whose love and support is a continual strength to me.

It is important for me to point out that this book emphasizes only one particular aspect of biblical teaching. It is as we grasp the breadth of truth in the teachings of Scripture that we find balance in our Christian lives. When we concentrate on one aspect of teaching to the exclusion of all others we move into extreme and error. Alongside the emphasis of this book we all need to grasp the necessity of being based in and dependent upon a body of fellow believers. The age of purely individualistic Christianity is over. We must find our place in the loving, caring fellowship of a Christian body. Then again, if we were to put all our emphasis on that we might well lose our dependence upon God as our heavenly Father.

So we need to know both the personal love of the Father and the corporate love of the family. Interestingly enough, when Jesus taught the disciples to pray he did not tell them to say 'my father' but 'our father'. I trust that, for all of us, that will become a growing reality in our lives.

BY WAY OF INTRODUCTION

Adventures in Faith

For most people it was a normal June afternoon. (In fact that isn't quite true as the sun was out and it was beautifully warm!) People were rushing to and fro in the sunshine. The characteristic smell of Smithfield meat market was strong in the air. It was a hive of activity, with men shouting and hurrying by, pushing their large carts, some loaded with meat and others empty. On the street as people wandered up and down you could see groups of nurses deep in conversation as they bustled along the pavement. This was a typical scene outside Bart's Hospital in London to which I had become familiar over the previous three years.

For me, though, as I wandered down the street, that day marked a major turning point in my life. It was one of those periods of time when I felt utterly alone. Alone because no other human being could stand where I was standing and come with me on a journey that I felt God had asked me to take. It wasn't that other people were not being asked to do specific things by God, or that they were not also finding their own personal struggles, but I knew that this was God dealing with me as an individual and that humanly I was alone at this point. It was the first time in my life that I really had to discover whether or not God was dependable, in a way that would cost me dearly if I had got it wrong.

A few minutes earlier I had made the final decision to leave medical school and had been to see the dean of the college. It was as if I had burned my bridges of human security.

I had become a Christian three years previously in my last year at school through the witness of a friend. It was a year later that I came to experience the power of the Holy Spirit in my life. Although I had given my life to Christ at school, it was not until the following summer that I was baptized in the Holy Spirit. My three years at medical school were marvellously exciting times. I suppose for everybody leaving school and going into a college situation or out into the world there are so many new and exciting discoveries. There was the tremendous freedom of being away from home and in London and with all the opportunities that opened up in front of us as young people.

The first two years were quite hard work and very academic, and since I am not the brightest thing on two legs I had to work reasonably hard to get through the exams. As I thought back over those years, there had been times of tremendous fun and also pain. There was all the excitement of new discoveries and of being a student and the early days of growth in my Christian life. But there were the difficult times too.

I remember one summer holiday I was driving back from the Isle of Man with a group of friends where we had been on a Pathfinder camp. As we drove down the M1 another car had a blow out and flew straight into us—turning the car I was driving over. Eventually it came to a standstill upside down in the fast lane of the motorway! I remember sitting there with a sense that this was the end of everything. But, as you will appreciate, it wasn't! There was obviously nobody behind and we were spared a big collision. Eventually we climbed out through the windows and all five of us in the car were unhurt, apart from one girl who had damaged her foot. God had wonderfully preserved us. I was taken in an ambulance to a nearby hospital with some of the others —including the girl who had been injured. When we arrived I found that the doctor on duty was somebody whom I had already got to know at medical school.

'Well,' he said, 'you were fortunate. You certainly got off better than your friend Bob.' Bob had been a fellow student who had become a Christian after six months at medical school and God had wonderfully worked in his life. 'What has happened to Bob? I asked. 'He is dead. He was killed in a motorbike accident last week.'

I was completely stunned. Not only by the casual way in which he had told me, but by the shock of losing someone who had become such a close friend. As I thought about it during the following days I realized that my own life had been spared, but for some reason Bob was gone. I was so grateful that he knew the Lord in a personal way and that we could be sure he had gone to be with him.

Even though I knew that to be true and that he was in a far better place, it raised all sorts of questions in my mind. These are questions that we all often ask, but there are no clear answers. He had only been married a few months. Why should God have allowed him to be killed? All I knew then and all I know now is that God is a caring God whose perspective of reality is so much bigger than ours, and that one day we will understand some of these harder things. I knew too, through that experience, that the life I did have was in God's hands and I didn't know how long I would be here. I had to determine to make sure I used my life fully for him.

After all, I knew I could have died on that day and so the life I had now was borrowed time. There is a sense in which this is true for every Christian. When we come to Christ it is as if we are dying and starting again. That is why the Christian life is not just a continuation of the old. It is the end of the old and the beginning of the new. We are all on borrowed time—every day is a gift from God, and needs to be used for him and with him. The reality of baptism is that we are to live as if we have died. Paul talked of 'living sacrifices'.

Hard times and good times. What fun we had on the wards as totally inexperienced and naive students! I never quite understood how they dared allow the likes of us to get anywhere near people who were genuinely ill! Actually, the medical care was really excellent despite our inexperience. A friend and I used to have competitions to see how much fruit and chocolate we could manage to persuade those dear patients to part with. On a good day we would end up quite sick!

During that time, however, I had a growing awareness that God's call for me was not in medicine but in some other form of full-time service. I listened to all the arguments for the need for Christians in medicine. I knew that many would go abroad as missionaries and help in far off countries using their medical skill and knowledge as a means of helping people, and as an opportunity to reach people in other countries for Christ. I knew all of that, but I knew too that God's call for me was different. I was very aware that it is not a good thing for a person to leave in the middle of a course, and would never encourage others to do it! It is all too easy to get out when the pressure comes, but I knew that I had gone through some of the worst exams and I had given it a whole year in which God could speak to me. It wasn't a rushed decision. He had confirmed his word to me again and again and I knew that I was taking the right step, but because of the potentially grave consequences I had to wait until I was absolutely sure before making such a decision.

As I stood there on the street on that June day, I knew I had said goodbye to a secure job and future, and what lay ahead seemed so uncertain and insecure. But I was sure in my heart that God had called me that way.

Through the encouragement of a Christian friend I had booked to go to the United States to work on a camp for two months, as I knew this would give me a good break. With the last remaining pounds of my grant I had put a deposit on the flight, but I still owed about fifty pounds. It was a very strange feeling to know that I had no money, no obvious future, and had left behind all the security I had previously known.

As I walked back along the street I saw a fellow student whom I knew well coming towards me, but I wasn't really sure I wanted to talk to anybody at that moment. Fortunately he didn't look like he was stopping for a conversation, but as he passed me he put an envelope in my hand, saying that what was enclosed was for me. Before I had time to make any comment, or talk to him further, he had gone on down the road. On opening it I found it to be full of cash—sufficient for the remainder of my fare and some spending money. I can remember standing there in the street amid the hustle and bustle with tears pouring down my face. It wasn't just gratitude for the money, although I was of course immensely grateful to him for giving it to me, but it was the overwhelming sense that God as my Father was caring for me and that this was just the beginning of so much more that he wanted to do. I knew that although the gift had come through human hands it was actually from the Father himself.

I spent most of my time at the camp washing dishes, which was hard work, but the experience was worth while—especially so because of the people I met. But this is not the time or place to write more of the extraordinary experiences during that summer. When I returned to England in September I went through a second period of real deep loneliness. I wasn't sure what I was going to do.

The strange thing was that before I went away, while I was staying in Birmingham, I had overheard some friends of mine saying that Jean Darnell was coming to Birmingham in September of that year. I had not the slightest idea who she was, where she came from or what she did, but in a strange way her name stuck in my mind. I knew that I needed to hear her. When I returned from America I really had no idea what I was going to do or where I would go, except for this one thought that I needed to go and hear this lady. So although these meetings were ten days away, I arranged to stay with some friends in Birmingham. I remember that period vividly as I sat day after day wondering what I was doing and whether I had misheard God. I can remember kneeling down one morning and crying out to God, 'Are you really with me? Do you really care?' Only a few minutes later I was told that two letters had arrived for me. The first was a letter from a person I had met in America, which had been forwarded from an address in London. As I read through the letter, the writer said he felt he should send me the words of a song based on Isaiah 41 that went something like this:

> Fear not I am with thee,
> O be not dismayed,
> For I am thy God,
> I will still give thee aid,

I will strengthen thee, help thee,
And cause thee to stand,
Upheld by my gracious omnipotent hand.

I opened the next letter which was from Lois, who was at that time my girlfriend and lived in London. She had written to say that the day before, God had really encouraged her with some verses from Isaiah 41 and she felt they were really for me. They were Isaiah 41:10, 'Fear not for I am with thee. . . .' Again I began to cry as I felt the loving hand of God the Father showing his care.

The following week, after one of Jean's meetings, I went to see her and she asked me what I wanted. I had to admit that I wasn't aware of any particular need and I didn't quite know why I should see her. But as we began to share, it was quite obvious why God had put us in touch with each other. She and her husband were starting a Bible school in Dorset. The opening day for the college was the following Monday. She had only one brochure left but that was all I needed!

I had been to America with Tony Dale, another medical student friend who had been on his vacation, and when we returned he went back to medicine and I to Birmingham. I decided on my way down to Poole that I would stop off to see Tony and share with him what I had decided to do. When I arrived in London I was amazed to find that he had decided to take two years out from medical school and go down to Dorset to a Bible college they were just starting! It was even more amazing to find out that there were only twelve students and that he and I had both had a call from God quite independently from one another. It was a wonderful little touch from God and we travelled down together. What a difference it makes having at least one other person with you. No wonder Jesus sent them out two by two.

Tony and I went looking for accommodation together and right from the start we learnt a great deal about God's provision. Somebody recommended that we visit a widow who lived near the centre of the town. They had heard that she might be willing to offer accommodation. We knocked on her door and she warmly welcomed us into the house. Much to our amazement she told us that the Lord had spoken to her some days before that there would be some people coming. She had moved out of the main bedroom into the back bedroom of her house and had put two single beds in the large front room. She told us that God had quite specifically impressed on her mind that two lodgers would be coming and so she wasn't very surprised to see us! We lived there with Mrs Samways for two years and it was a tremendous experience of learning to trust God in so many large and small ways.

We worked during the day and went to college at night. We found a job at the local hospital washing intravenous bottles and making up solutions. It was rather humbling for someone who had been a medical student, striding up and down the ward in his white coat thinking he knew everything, to find himself washing bottles in a pharmacy! I was by now wondering whether washing up was likely to be my career!

As we shared the job, we only had to work half a day each, but it meant that the pay was rather low. We were paid on a Friday and always ran out of money by the following Tuesday. We had to live every week from Tuesday to Friday depending on God to provide our needs. We had some very interesting experiences and it certainly wasn't easy all the time. We had some hard times and some good times, but each was an experience of learning. When God did provide it was so clear that it was him that we were able to cope with the times when we had less.

On one occasion I invited another student around for a meal. There was no food in the house so our landlady took sympathy on her and fed her and we went without! I am not sure what we learned, but I don't think God felt we went through great hardship by missing one meal.

I vividly remember sitting down one day and all we had was half a ham sandwich between us. It really was the straw that broke the camel's back. I can vividly remember banging my sandwich on the table and shouting, 'If this is the best you can do I don't think much of it. I thought you were meant to be providing for us and we end up with a quarter of a ham sandwich. Is this supposed to be the abundant life!' I don't think God took my threats too seriously and looking back on it I know that was a very important experience.

Being a fairly undisciplined person, one of the marvellous things was that God had put me with somebody who was very disciplined in his life. Tony helped me with Bible reading and learning verses as well as other disciplines of the Christian life. It was there that I learned for the first time the importance of tithing our income. We had two jam jars on our chest of drawers. One was for the tithe and one was for money that we had in hand. On many occasions our current account jar was empty and our tithe jar was stuffed with pound notes. It was sometimes very difficult and we were very tempted to borrow from God occasionally!

We saw so many specific answers to prayer which were really exciting and convincing for us. We learnt about faith at college each evening and had to experience it during the day. Tony didn't like to spend money on himself, and refused to buy the new shoes he desperately needed. I prayed one day very specifically that somehow we would be able to buy him some new ones. The very next day somebody came up to him and handed him some money and said, 'Tony, this money is specifically for you to buy shoes.' It took a long time to convince him that I hadn't arranged the whole thing!

On one occasion I wanted to attend a rally in London for which it was necessary to have tickets. Some months before I was told it was completely booked out and there was a long waiting list, so the chances of getting in were almost nil. I felt very disappointed about it, but when I prayed I felt that God was encouraging me to go. I told Lois that I would be coming up to London and we would go to this event, but I had no idea how we would actually get in.

It was a damp, cold morning when Tony and I (Tony was going to London for something else) stood on the main road outside Poole, hitching a lift to London. The first lift we got took us about ten miles up the road and we stood again by the roadside. Almost immediately a minibus stopped and offered us a lift. We found that it was going to London, having set out from Cornwall, and so we were able to get a lift the whole way. The interesting thing was that there were two empty spaces in the minibus. We discovered in the course of conversation that this particular group were on their way to the very meeting I wanted to go to. It was quite remarkable to discover that the night before they had had two cancellations and so had two spare tickets for this event and were wondering what to do with them. On top of that there were two lunches which were most agreeable! To be on the right part of the road between Cornwall and London at the specific time that two tickets came driving past seemed much more than a coincidence!

It was on occasions such as this that I began to see the hand of a heavenly Father in such a loving, tender, caring way. Along the way, through the difficulties and the joys, he was teaching the reality that he was a Father who cares and he wanted me to grow up as a child trusting him and depending upon him, yet not spoilt. I was never to receive everything I wanted, but I had to learn the basic ingredients of trust. The whole of life is a process of learning. As soon as you have learnt one lesson God takes you on to another. I had to learn to trust him for small things; later we were to be involved in seeing provision on a large scale not only for our own needs but those of others.

It would be easy to sit down and write volumes about God's miraculous provision in both our lives at that time and increasingly over the years which have followed. Although that would be an exciting thing to do, I don't feel this is the place for it as it easily draws attention to the writer instead of the One who provides. Everybody has a story. Mine is certainly not special. I was with a group of young people recently, and we went round the room asking each to share the testimony of what God had done in their lives. It was breathtaking to listen to the variety of amazing ways in which God had stepped into each of these lives and demonstrated his love for them and his desire to be their God and Father. Every Christian is a living miracle and testimony to God's amazing love. I like to ask people how they came to find Christ. Each time it underlines God's incredible love and reminds us that whenever a man is seeking God he will find him because God is looking for those who are seeking.

I find in my own experience that many of the things God does in our lives are very personal and between ourselves and him. Although it is tempting to want to share them, they remain among the things that are private. You and God know them, and they are not to be painted on a billboard or proclaimed from the rooftops. It isn't God's intention that everything he does in our lives is shouted out, for many things are intimate expressions of love between God the Father and his children. Those intimate things are special and they need to remain that way. Maybe heaven will give us an opportunity for sharing them.

I discovered too that God's guidance often changes as we grow up in the Christian life. Early on we see very specific changes in circumstances and all our prayers seem to be answered easily. It is as if God takes particular care in those early stumbling stages as we learn to walk with him. But as we grow he expects us to learn to hear his voice more clearly. It is the difference between knowing what to do because the door in front of you is open, and the later stage of being told to open and go through a closed door. As we grow up we have to learn to hear God's voice more clearly, and become more mature in our relationship with him. The Lord, though, only expects us to respond according to our stage of growth.

Can you imagine a father watching his little child learning to walk? As the child gets half way across the room and falls over, the father won't be angry with the child, nor tell him how stupid he is and that he ought to know better. Most fathers would rush to their children and pick them up thrilled with the fact that they walked as far as they did, and then encourage them on their way. We are all at different stages in our Christian life. God is encouraging us to learn to walk and to trust him and to know that he is with us every step of the way.

The truth is that we only see a fraction of what God does for us. When I give my boys gifts, or do something specific, they are grateful. Most of what I do indirectly for them is totally unseen. So with God, his daily protection, provision and leading is mostly unseen. How hard it must be to have us complaining about his apparent lack of love in one area when he can see all he is doing for us.

> If I rise on the wings of the dawn,
> if I settle on the far side of the sea,
> even there your hand will guide me,
> your right hand will hold me fast.
>
> (Psalm 139:9–10, NIV)

> The steps of a man are from the Lord,
> And he establishes him in whose way he delights;
> though he fall, he shall not be cast headlong,
> for the Lord is the stay of his hand.
>
> (Psalm 37:23)

The whole purpose of learning to trust God in this way is not just for our own benefit. It is in order that we may be free from worry over petty concerns to give ourselves to God's service. There is so much that God has for each of us to do in helping and serving others. We must break free from the pattern of life becoming just a mass of personal concerns about personal needs. When we trust him for the small details, we can start to meet the needs of others.

I

The Prodigal World

We live at a time in history like no other, for, as we are constantly reminded, we have the potential to destroy the entire human race in a matter of moments. We live every day in the light of that possibility and it is no wonder there is so little optimism about the future. The secular prophets, disregarded by most of us because of the hopelessness of their predictions, tell us that we are within a generation or two of the climax of history. If you listen carefully to those who study the environment they tell us of a growing lack of natural resources and of the destructive elements that man has put into the world which will eventually destroy us. They see only a horrifying future and the only answer put forward by man to solve his own dilemma would require such a reversal of human nature that it is always dismissed as an impossibility.

Conflict and poverty

It is a world full of conflict. On almost every continent there are nations fighting each other and hundreds are dying or being mutilated daily. The world is divided between the rich and the poor: those in the West have excessive amounts of food and material resources, while a large section of the world starves. Ignorance of the problem is no longer an excuse since we have all been exposed to the reality of this present horror. Man has within his grasp the possibility of providing enough food to feed the world, and yet he has chosen not to do so.

In a recent survey people were asked on the streets of Britain whether they would be prepared to take a drop in income in order to help provide for the poor of the world. The majority replied that they wouldn't be prepared to do that! That is a symptom of the sickness of our world. Politicians have to promise us growth and prosperity if they are going to win votes. Isn't that one of the obscenities of Western society?

Confusion

We live in a morally confused world in which we destroy tens of thousands of unborn babies, even though there are large numbers of couples unable to have children who would like to adopt them. The younger generation look to their parents for direction and see hypocrisy. They hear one thing and observe another. The young people always get the blame for the ills of society and yet in reality such things as exploitation of sex and sale of drugs are motivated by large financial stakes. The older generation use the vulnerability of the young to make money, and then leave them in a moral vacuum.

We have taught a whole generation that man's evolution can be explained in purely natural terms and by implication disregard the relevance of God or any need for him. Then we are surprised that, having taught people that they are merely animals, they then proceed to live like them. In the sixties people were talking in positive terms about hope for mankind, but these voices seem to be silenced today.

Chance

It was assumed that as Christianity declined in Britain and the West, it would be paralleled by a rise in what is called scientific rationalism. These were the theories of the sociologists of the sixties, but in fact what has happened is that the decline has been followed by a rise in superstition. G. K. Chesterton once said, 'When people stop believing in God, they do not start believing in nothing, they start believing in anything!' So today this generation, which has apparently turned its back on God, has continued to seek answers beyond a natural world and has therefore looked to forms of occultism. No wonder on television, the radio, the press and every other form of media we are bombarded with horoscopes. Astrology has become a central topic of daily conversation for many. Young people have turned to ouija boards and other forms of occult activity. Is it any wonder in such a lost world that so vast a number of people attend their doctor to receive pills and tablets to cope with depression and anxiety?

Change

We live in a world where the rate of change increases at an alarming speed. The progress in scientific discovery and technological improvement moves forward at a devastating rate. Anything we buy today is immediately obsolete as a more advanced form will be produced by tomorrow. This increases the tremendous instability of our society as we live in an instant world that wants instant things. We are not sure about tomorrow so we want the best today.

We are becoming an increasingly depersonalized society where men and women are categorized by numbers instead of names. The micro chip revolution has only just begun and will have far-reaching consequences on every area of life, both for good and bad. In its early days it has brought in new forms of entertainment such as 'space invaders' and the home computer. Children sit for hours, no longer having to relate to another human being but only to a machine. With home video and teletext people can stay at home and receive all the information they need, without having to go out and meet with others. A friend of mine in the United States said recently, 'In our neighbourhood, which is fairly wealthy, we used at least to see the neighbours walk to the car each day! Now everybody has an automatic garage door and they drive straight into the house!' Increasingly few neighbourhoods are real communities in the accepted sense of that word. There is such mobility in our society that nobody stays in one place long enough to build up a strong community relationship.

Where are we going?

And so we could go on and on. It all leads to a lost generation. The great characteristic of our world is fear which stems from a deep sense of insecurity. We do not know where we came from. We do not know where we are going. We do not know who we really are. The things that used to make us feel secure are suddenly becoming so unsure. At least we used to have relationships and marriages that held together, but now it is increasingly few that really last.

In his excellent book *Finding Faith,* Andrew Knowles asked the question, 'Who am I?'

> I am a mystery. I wake up in the morning. I find myself the sole occupant of a complex, sensitive, and extremely useful

body. I am also the proud owner of an intricate, imaginative, and highly resourceful brain. Everything about me is unique; my face, my fingerprints, my self.

I am alive. I develop. I grow. So does a vegetable. But I am more than a vegetable. Vegetables don't fall in love, or read the paper, or go on holiday....

I am a body with a brain; an animal. But I am more than an animal.

Animals don't peer through telescopes, or send birthday cards, or play chess, or cook....

Surely I have a dimension that animals and vegetables lack? After all, a carrot is oblivious of the size of Jupiter. A cow cares nothing for the speed of light.

But I am in a different class. I observe and appreciate. I create and I choose. I am aware. I criticise. Sometimes I even criticise myself!

I am different. I am mankind. In fact the Bible says I am Godkind.

The Bible tells me that I am like God; that I exist in something of the way that God exists, that I am aware in some of the ways that God is aware. And although I cannot prove it, the idea that I am made in the image of God makes more sense than all the other views put together. Indeed, it helps me to put the other views together, and see them and myself, as a whole. I am a person created by God unique in the entire universe and in the whole of history and I know it! [*Finding Faith,* Lion Publishing 1983.]

Fear

One of the great destructive forces in our world today is fear. It is expressed in so many different ways.

Fear of death

Death is a subject that most of us will not talk about although it happens to be the one event that is experienced by every single person. George Bernard Shaw once said, 'Death is the ultimate statistic—one out of one dies!' But death for us all means an end to what we know and it has to be faced individually and without the help of others. So we have to leave behind our relationships, our material possessions, our positions in life, and all those other things which offer us a degree of security.

Fear of the future

Because of the uncertainties of the world we can live continually in fear of what the future holds. So many of the things we take for granted such as employment and good relationships can no longer be treated as stable factors in our lives. Very few people are talking optimistically any more about the years ahead as it is impossible to see how human beings can improve the world in which we live.

Fear of disease

There is anxiety that at any time disease could strike and our health be impaired which would mean that our lives would not be as full as they are now.

Fear of circumstances

None of us knows what is going to happen and what things could change or influence our present situation. It is easy to feel like a little boat in the midst of a large ocean—tossed around and vulnerable.

Fear of others

It is amazing how many of us change our behaviour in order to receive the approval of others—for example, the way we talk, the things we wear. The things we say and do are not done because that is what we want to do, but ultimately because we want to please other people. We are so afraid of what others will think that we can only rarely be ourselves.

Fear of failure

This drives us in one of two directions. It either makes us incredibly busy and active in order to achieve: we rush around either at work or at home in order to do enough to show that we have succeeded. Or it takes the opposite direction—we drift into total apathy. We find that we won't attempt anything because we are afraid we will fail. We have failed in the past and we may well do again so it is better not to try.

And so these fears go on and take away from us the real joy of living.

A new way of living

C. S. Lewis once said, 'If I find in myself a desire which no experience in this world can satisfy, the most probable explanation is that I was made for another world.' When Jesus burst onto the scene he came to tell us that in fact we *are* made for another world! We are made for a whole different kind of experience. We are intended to live hand in hand with God. We are made to be alive physically, mentally and spiritually, and to be continually in touch with the Maker and Creator of the universe. God never intended us to be as we are today; we are experiencing the results of man's choice to live and to dominate his world without God. That is why when Jesus came to the world he did not come to bring in a new self-improvement scheme. Nor did he come to give us more rules or to set us an example. He came to tell us about a kingdom. A kingdom in which men could rediscover where they came from, who they are, and where they are going. It is a kingdom in which everybody matters and in which each is important and known by name. It is a kingdom of peace and joy and hope. It's one of power and reality.

When Jesus walked this earth he expressed in his own life the nature of this kingdom. Here was a man, to all intents and purposes an apparently ordinary man, eating and drinking, walking this earth and yet expressing in his life a whole new concept of living. The infinite Creator God became a part of his own creation! Jesus was God in human form. Through his life on earth he showed us how we are intended to be. He lived on earth but he lived quite differently from any other man. In his values, in his understanding and in his lifestyle he expressed a completely different form of living than had ever been seen before. And he came to tell us that this is not only how we are meant to live, but how we actually *can* live. He came not to tantalize us but to offer us the opportunity to live in that kingdom.

In the kingdom of God there is no need to fear. The ultimate enemy, death, has been overcome by Jesus on the cross and he comes to give us an assurance that death is now only a doorway to a greater life with him. Entrance into this kingdom brings us into a place of complete security as we see the God who is the Creator of this universe in control of the circumstances of our lives. He takes hold of us and walks with us into the future. He enables us to be free to be ourselves and to know that we no longer have to strive to succeed. We can live with him in a relationship of peace and acceptance. Supremely he tells us who we really are and gives us our identity. We are not a number but a name! No wonder Jesus said, 'The thief comes only to steal and kill and destroy; I have come that they may have life, and have it to the full. I am the good shepherd; I know my sheep and my sheep know me—just as the Father knows me and I know the Father—and I lay down my life for the sheep' (John 10:10, 14–15, NIV).

New beginning

Jesus made it very clear that there is only one way to enter into this kingdom. He called it new birth. Before it can affect our outward living, the kingdom of God must first touch our inner experience. Therefore we need to begin by receiving new life. This life is given to us in the person of the Holy Spirit who comes to live within us. He then wants to live his life out through us. In order to receive the Spirit of God we must first turn from our old life and acknowledge our need of forgiveness which is freely available because of what Jesus did on the cross.

Right across the world today there are increasing numbers of people who are discovering this new life in Christ. Of course there are still large numbers who have yet to hear of this kingdom and all that it offers. What is written in the following pages will, I hope, be of some help both to those who are seeking, and to those who've already entered the kingdom of God but who are still living in a certain degree of insecurity and fear. Sadly there are many of us who are not yet enjoying the full inheritance that is ours. This should not fill us with guilt but rather encourage us to go on to discover all that God has for us.

2

The Father God

In order to understand the fatherhood of God we need to look into some of the misconceptions and misunderstandings about God.

What is he like?

What you think about God determines how you live. What a man says he believes and what he actually believes may be two different things, and the way you discover which is true is to observe how he lives and how he behaves. For example, if a car salesman tells you that Fords are the best cars on the road and then you find that he drives a Vauxhall, I doubt if what he says is actually what he believes! If a man says that a particular chair will hold his weight but refuses to sit on it, I doubt that he really believes it. If a man says it is not going to rain and he goes out with his umbrella, he actually believes it may rain. These may sound rather trite examples, but they illustrate that the whole of our life is made up of action based on belief.

Faith

Faith is the living out of belief and is based on trust. This applies to the atheist and the Christian alike. The atheist may believe that there is no God and lives on that basis. The Christian trusts in Jesus and his word.

Now faith of itself, in the above sense, is not a specifically Christian attribute. But faith in God as a loving heavenly Father expressed in our daily lives, is what Christianity is all about. The degree of faith which we exercise will be related to how we understand the nature of God and our attitude to his word. If we are going to trust him we have first to believe that he is there at all. Then if we are going to put a lot of trust in him we have to believe in his ability to hear us, to respond to us, his power to act and his desire to do so. The more of these attributes we believe about God the more willing we will be to trust him.

The whole of life is made up of faith. We catch a particular bus because we believe that number bus will get us where we want to go. I often hear people say, 'Well, I'll believe in God if you can prove it.' I have never heard a person stand at the bus stop and say to the bus driver, 'If you can prove that this bus will get me to my destination then I'll get on it!' They observe the facts in front of them and draw certain conclusions on that basis. They get on the bus because they believe that the evidence they have is reasonable. There is an element of faith involved, faith working with reason.

A man turns on the television to watch a certain programme because he believes the *Radio Times* is telling the truth. He goes to a meeting because he believes the people who said the meeting would happen are trustworthy, therefore it will happen. He doesn't require further proof before he takes that step. He acts in faith based on trust in another individual's word. That faith expressed in this situation is dependent upon the amount of trust in those individuals. That is why the faith talked about in the New Testament is not an enormous step forward from what we already know. It simply means that we trust in the words of Jesus and what he had to teach us about God. When we are dealing in the realm of God we cannot rely on our senses. We can't touch him, see him, hear him, smell him, or taste him. We are entirely dependent upon his word.

Angry old man

For many people, often due to the portrayal of Christianity through the ages by the church and lately through the media, there is a belief that God's character is a somewhat austere and oppressive one. If you believe that God is like that then your life will be lived accordingly. The most natural tendency will be not to allow God's involvement in any real issue in your life because he may take away the things you most appreciate and enjoy. Of course, the very opposite is true in fact. God created life, and the world he made for us to live in he made to be good. All the good experiences of life have their roots in God. Can you imagine the record in the book of Genesis reading: 'And God saw all that he had made and behold it was very boring. It was dull and monotonous and dreary and God put man on the face of the earth!' When God made it he saw that it was good. It is man who has come and taken these things and used them to excess and therefore spoiled them. But God intended us to enjoy this world to the full. We only have to look at Jesus to find out what God is really like and how to get the most out of life.

There are, of course, many religious people who

believe this. These are the folk who attend church and are involved in a great deal of religious activity but have no real personal experience of God. Their understanding of God will vary from person to person; however, predominantly it will be of a God who exists but who is not particularly active in his world. They feel he must be pleased with them because of their religious observance and activity and feel sure of their place in heaven, but would be amazed if God were actually to intervene in their own lives.

Paternal Grandfather

There are those who feel God is weak and anaemic and continually oozes a sentimental form of love. If you believe this about God you will live accordingly. It will mean that you don't actually care about how you live because you have the feeling that somehow it will work out in the end and 'God loves us all anyway doesn't he'! People often say, 'After all God is a loving God and he forgives us so it doesn't really matter what I do.'

The idea of a loving God came from the Bible so we need to go back and see what the Bible really does teach about God. We will discover that, while he is a God of love, this does not preclude his being a God of judgement, holiness and righteousness.

Saviour

Those who have begun the Christian life are those who have not only believed that Jesus is the Saviour but have taken an active step and trusted him to take away their sin. They have understood the saving love of God, and have seen their own inadequacy and failure and begun to grasp the importance of the death of Christ on the cross for them. They have received the forgiveness of God and therefore entered into a relationship with him, and have been filled with the Holy Spirit and are aware of the power of God in their lives.

But even within the family of God there are different understandings of the nature of God. This is seen not by what people say but by the way they live. There are those, for example, who look on God as a divine boss into whose employ they have come.

Divine employer

There may be some who have become Christians to avoid hell and assume that the Christian life has to be endured between now and their impending death! If you do actually believe God is like some sort of divine employer, then all of your life will be an attempt to try and serve him and to work hard in order to gain his pleasure and approval. It is so easy to begin the Christian life understanding that it is based on the free gift of God, provided purely out of God's goodness, but then to drift into a life which denies that very liberating truth. We so quickly take on an attitude which says that if we do enough and work hard enough then we will make the grade and God will be pleased. Our churches today know many like this, people who feel that their acceptance has something to do with their behaviour and their religious activity. Paul says: 'For freedom Christ has made us free.' It is easy to fail to experience that freedom. Most of us don't like to admit that we come into this category, but so much of our lives are full of what we ought to do or what we should do and therefore our activity is a result of our obligation.

When Jesus told the story of the prodigal son he finished by talking about an older brother. The words of the brother to the father are very telling, 'Look! For so many years I have been serving you and I have never neglected a command of yours and yet....' He had never really enjoyed the benefits of being a son because he had the attitude that he had to work for his father in order to please him. Of course, Jesus was speaking directly to the Pharisees and the religious leaders of his day.

We have invented a new form of pharisaism in the church which is there primarily because of our misunderstanding of the character and the nature of God. Of course it was right that the elder brother worked and was involved in his father's property. In the same way God wants us to obey him and do the things that please him. But God's approval and his acceptance of us are purely because we are his children brought about by an act of his love and grace. Our obedience is our response to him as a way of telling him that we love him. We are not working *in order to* gain approval; rather we serve him *from* a position of being approved in Christ.

Faith means taking the word of God and putting our trust in him. God's word as expressed in the Bible is quite clear about the nature of God as Lord and Father.

Father

In the period before Jesus came to live on earth there was a growing tendency to have a more and more abstract idea of God. The scribes in their writings and their interpretation of the Scriptures removed God further and further from real contact with man and the world. This meant that religious experience became more and more dominated by an outward show of religious duty. When Jesus came into our world he brought a whole new concept of God. No wonder the religious leaders hated him. Here was a man who not only taught about God but obviously experienced him in a personal way. His life was full of vitality, but at the same time he seemed to walk roughshod over all the ceremony and religious observances of the Pharisees. Jesus came to describe to us the real nature and character of God and tell us about our relationship with him. As you read through the pages of the New Testament you cannot miss the fact that Jesus' underlying and predominant teaching was that God's character is the character of a father.

The first recorded sentence of Jesus is in Luke 2:49 where he refers to God as his Father. 'Why are you searching for me? Didn't you know I had to be in my Father's house?' (NIV). Twenty years later, on the cross, Jesus' last words before his death are recorded in Luke 23:46, 'Father, into your hands I commit my spirit' (NIV). Whenever the personal relationship between himself and God was involved, Jesus always referred to 'the Father'.

Jesus did not use the phrases that the Pharisees used to describe God. Such expressions as 'the blessed one', 'the holy one' and other such abstract phrases were never part of Jesus' vocabulary. Even when he did call God 'holy' or 'righteous', it was as he addressed him as 'holy Father' and 'righteous Father' (John 17:11, 25). It is quite clear from his teaching that he believed God's character was of a father and that God was his Father. The amazing thing is that he went on to say to his disciples that God was also their Father. So when he taught them to pray, he told them to say 'Our Father', and in Matthew 6:32 he refers to 'your heavenly Father...'.

In John's gospel the word 'Father' comes ninety times, in Luke seventeen times, in Mark five times, and in Matthew forty-five times. The subject on which Jesus claimed to possess unique knowledge was the character of God, and he chose to describe that character in terms of fatherhood. In fact, in the teachings of Jesus there were two main strands. First, he talked about the kingdom of God. Interwoven in this teaching of the kingdom he described the character of God as a father. This is because it is only when we come into an understanding of the kingdom that we can really know what it means to know God as Father.

Back to the garden

The easiest way to understand the relationship between these two truths is to go right back to the very beginning. In Genesis 1 and 2 the writer paints a beautiful picture of man living in complete harmony with God and with creation. Here he is with dominion over all the world and everything that is in it. He is completely free, and is living in a relationship with God that is close and intimate, and provides all the security and protection as well as the provision that he needs. Here is the perfect father-child relationship.

In the midst of it we are told that God had put a tree in the garden from which Adam and Eve were not to eat. The type of this tree and the nature of its fruit are really irrelevant. The purpose of it is that while they continued not to eat of that tree they were living in submission to God's authority. This was not an oppressive obedience. After all, they had the freedom to eat of every other tree that there was. But it was a continual sign of their commitment to God. By not eating of it they acknowledged continually that they were being obedient to him. That is the nature of the kingdom of God.

They enjoyed all the benefits of being true children of God because they lived under his authority and therefore his protection and care. But when the great deception took place and man chose to move outside of that authority and sought to be his own master, he not only lost all his freedom but became a slave to his own environment. He moved outside of the protection and the warm, close, intimate fellowship that he had once had.

That is the state of things today. It is ironic that man is seeking freedom and security but doesn't want to know God and so ends up in terrible slavery and bondage. If only he could put himself under God's authority he would receive real freedom. Such is the nature of the mass seduction mankind has swallowed.

When Jesus came to talk about the kingdom he was telling us that man can again come into that relationship with God whereby he submits his life and his will to God, and by so doing no longer loses his freedom but gains it. By doing that he enters into a relationship with God that is intimate and close, warm and protected. In Matthew 5 Jesus made it quite clear that the way to fully discover the security of having God as a father was to 'seek first the kingdom of God'. In other words if we put ourselves under the authority and the leadership of King Jesus, we will automatically discover the relationship of God the Father in our lives.

What Jesus means by the term 'Father' can be learned from his words and his life. It is quite clear that he used the terms to describe the character of God. For example as he taught that it is the nature of a father to give good gifts to his children, so it is the very nature of God to give good gifts to those who are his (Luke 11:13). In other words, the term fatherhood describes what God actually is in himself.

It isn't concerned just with his relationship to man but it underlines his very spirit and character. So it is that in the Old Testament God had on a number of occasions described himself as a father to Israel (Hosea 11:1; Deuteronomy 8:5; 32:6).

Daddy

In his commentary on Romans, F. F. Bruce has this to say about the use of the word *Abba*.

> *Abba* is an Aramaic word which came to be used among the Jews (and is used to this day among Hebrew speaking families) and was a familiar term by which children addressed their father. In Mark 14:36 Jesus is represented as using it in his prayer in Gethsemane. The significance of this lies in the fact that *Abba* was not and is not a term used by Jews when addressing God as their father. But the fact that this Aramaic word found its way into the worshipping vocabulary of the Gentile churches strongly suggests that it was used in this way by Jesus. Mark 14:36 confirms this. There is a strong presumption too that when Jesus taught his disciples to begin their prayers with 'Father, hallowed be thy name' (Luke 11:2), the word he used for father was *Abba* . This sufficiently explains the passage of the Aramaic term into the usage of the Greek-speaking Christians. [*The Epistle of Paul to the Romans,* IVP 1983.]

Isn't it incredible that Jesus suggested that we call God, the Creator of the universe, by that intimate title 'Daddy'!

If you can cope with a little bit of old English it is worth reading what Martin Luther wrote on the word *Abba*:

> This is but a little word, and yet not withstanding it comprehendeth all things. The mouth speaketh not, but the affection of the heart speaketh after this manner. Although I be oppressed with anguish and terror on every side, and seem to be forsaken and utterly cast away from thy presence, yet I am thy child, and thou art my father for Christ's sake; I

am beloved because of the beloved. Wherefore this little word 'Father' conceived affectually in the heart passeth all the eloquence of Demosthenes, Cicero, and of the most eloquent rhetoricians that ever were in the world. This matter is not expressed in words, but with groanings, which groanings cannot be uttered with any groanings or eloquence, for no tongue can express them.

Jesus rocked the religious teaching of his day. The scribes had declared that God was in the seventh heaven. Jesus taught that he was near. The scribes taught that God was really only primarily concerned with outward ordinances and practices. Jesus taught that he was full of love and cares firstly for the heart of man. To the Pharisees God was a God to the religious people. To Jesus he desired to be a friend to sinners, and a father to all who would come to him.

Jesus expressed in his very life what it meant to be the Son of God and thereby showed the way for all who were to follow him as 'sons of God'. He expressed life, joy, vitality, holiness and goodness. He lived his life in obedience to what he knew the Father wanted. He wasn't anxious, full of fear, burdened, weighed down, oppressed, negative—but full of hope with a gloriously positive attitude to life. He was free and lived a life as we know it should be lived. He wasn't hampered or oppressed by a sense of religious duty. He was rejected by the leaders of his day and eventually by the people. But he wasn't afraid to say what he knew to be true. His security lay in knowing God his Father loved him and cared for him, and because of this tremendous sense of security he was not afraid of being rejected.

He was a man who didn't have to say things purely to please other people. He wasn't always wanting people to think well of him so that he could have a good position in their eyes. He wasn't seeking status. He didn't want to succeed in the normal sense of the word. His only desire in life was to be obedient to his Father. And as he walked through Galilee and then eventually into Jerusalem, we see in this man a tremendous sense of knowing exactly who he was, where he came from and where he was going.

What about us?

Jesus came to tell us that God's character is one of a father and he wants us to relate to him in this way. We have seen that what we believe about God determines how we live, but how are we going to decide what we believe about God? Are we going to look to our own opinions and ideas? Are we going to listen to the philosophers of our day? Are we even going to listen to the religious teachers? Surely the most authoritative person to speak about the nature of God is Jesus himself. And if Jesus taught that this is how God is, surely it is a sound basis for our belief.

When we begin to grasp this essential nature and character of God it must revolutionize our lives. When it dawns on us that to become a Christian is actually to enter into a relationship with the living God in the same way that a father has a relationship with his son—or as Paul puts it in Romans and Galatians, 'We are adopted into the family,'—this fact will change every aspect of our lives. What Jesus came to tell us was not that we have to imagine this is what God is like and somehow convince ourselves of the truth of it, but that we are to receive it as the very truth itself. It is not a wild fantasy, an extravagant idea, but it is the truth about God. We are free to receive it or reject it. We can enter into that relationship or stay removed from it. We can live in the reality of that truth or ignore it.

The truth about God will never change, but our response to that truth is the variable factor. Jesus told us that the truth would make us free and we must receive this truth not only with our minds but with our hearts. Can you be anything but free knowing the Creator of the universe is your Dad?

A choice

As Christians we have a choice. We can begin by saying, 'If God is a father...' then weigh every circumstance to see if it bears out this fact. When it doesn't and we feel low we are faced with the feeling that God does not care after all. When things do go well and life is good we are full of how wonderful God is towards us. If you live like that then you will be like a little boat tossed about on the sea and your life will be continually up and down.

But there is another way. That is to begin by saying, 'God is my Father and I have become his child.' Thus in every circumstance of life, good or bad, convenient or inconvenient, we are able to say with utter conviction that God is at work in each of these situations and is in control of all that is going on. It may not change the situation, but it will surely change the heart. It is in this second attitude to life that peace of heart grows and develops. It is not just wishful thinking because it is based upon God's word and the clear teaching of Jesus. Usually, too, we can look back and see with hindsight that in fact everything worked out for the best.

But we do have a choice. These are two radically different attitudes to life. And all of us who are Christians must choose which path we are going to take. If you decide on the second you will have chosen freedom.

God's perspective

So much of what we do and say is as a result of looking at everything from our own viewpoint. It is time we began to see things from God's angle. According to his revelation in the Scriptures, he sees us as children whom he loves. When we begin to see ourselves in that light we will come into a new place of peace and security. Again, the choice is between being dictated to by our feelings or asking the question, 'How does God feel?' Either we can say, 'I don't feel God loves me,' or we can believe God's statement when he says, 'I love you deeply.' When we start to see ourselves as God sees us we will begin to experience so much more of what he wants for us in our lives.

> How great is the love the Father has lavished on us, that we should be called children of God! *And that is what we are*!
>
> Dear friends, *now we are* children of God, and what we will be has not yet been made known (1 John 3:1–2, NIV, italics mine).

3

The Father's Heart

'This is hurting me more than it is hurting you.' Have you ever had that said to you? I don't know if you are anything like me, but it was one of the expressions I found very difficult to believe as a child! It seemed to be one of those things parents always said, but the reality of a red-hot and stinging part of my anatomy didn't encourage me to believe there was much truth in the statement.

But as a parent I have discovered otherwise. A child thinks and behaves as a child and can only look at the world from his own perspective. Therefore as a child of God it is difficult to understand fully the concept of what it means for God to be a father. But as a natural parent you can really begin to feel from a father's viewpoint and therefore know something of the father heart of God which it is impossible to understand purely on an intellectual level. It is possible to grasp it objectively with the mind, but it only really makes an impact on your life when it is a heart experience. God is a God who has feelings and he is longing for us to enter into and experience those feelings with him.

We gain much more understanding of the realities of life and much more motivation for our spiritual growth when we try to enter into the feelings of God. The Bible is a book which expresses very deeply what God feels for his world and for his people. We only have to read the prophets to understand something of the depth of God's emotions regarding his own creation. The prophets knew the very heart of God. God is not like a machine which has made something then looks at it purely from an academic and objective level. He has a heart and is therefore able to grieve, to be sad, to be happy and to be glad. It is always important to ask the question, 'How does God feel about this situation?'

I know that having children of my own has revolutionized my understanding of God's relationship with me and others of his children. This is not to advocate that everybody needs to rush out and have children in order to understand God, for God can reveal these truths through revelation to our spirits, but we need to grasp and realize for ourselves the depth of the feeling of the heart of God. Fatherhood is not just a biological state—it is an expression of relationship.

Let me add here that it would be foolish to base my understanding of God purely on my own experience of fatherhood. After all, my human fatherhood is tainted with all sorts of inadequate human feelings. The Bible tells me that man is made in the image of God, and therefore I can believe that much of what I experience in my relationship with my own children is merely a reflection of what God feels towards his.

When a person falls in love and gets married he has a special relationship with his wife. But when the couple have children, the relationship with the children, although equally a relationship of love, is of a different order. This is primarily because those children are an extension of the parents themselves. They are part of them, they come from them, so there is a very close link between the parent and the child.

Remembering that the experience of human fatherhood is really only a shadow of what God feels, let me outline some of the things I have experienced as a father.

Firstly, although I have two children I find I can love both of my children with all of my love. I don't apportion my love between my children. I have a friend who has seven children and he would honestly be able to say that he loves each of his children with all of his love. He doesn't love them with a seventh of his love or a part of his love, but all of his love. In the same way it is true to say that God loves each of us with all of his love. Every one of us receives the same amount of love from God. We may please him or displease him to different degrees, depending on our response to him, but his love for each of us is unchanging. It may be difficult to understand and grasp this fact, but it is true. I don't divide my love between my children and neither does God divide his love between his children. His whole heart is expressed in love to each one of us.

Having said that, parents may relate to their children in different ways and God's love for all of us does not mean he will treat us all in the same way. If God deals with me differently from you, it doesn't mean he loves me less or more than you.

Now, I think my children are absolutely fantastic. This is not to say they are necessarily well behaved all the time, or that they are clean and tidy, or that they are quiet, but I love them because they are my children. Before I was married, or before I had children, I remember going to people's homes and finding that one of the things they wanted to do was to bring out photo albums of their growing children. They would move from one page to another with increasing delight as they showed me these pictures. To them they were the most wonderful children in the whole world and every new step they took was a major landmark. To me they were children much like any other children. I am afraid I could never get terribly excited about looking at pictures of other people's children. Meeting these children was all right, but only in small doses. But now I have children of my own it is different. Come to my home and I am quite likely to make sure you sit down and look at photographs of my children! And I shall be very upset if you don't think they are wonderful. I look at them in a totally different light from anybody else, except their mother of course. I get excited about every development and change. I shall want you to meet them, get to know them and share my joy in them!

I remember once going to hospital with a friend to visit his wife and their newborn daughter. When we arrived he was most excited and picked up this tiny, red-faced, wrinkled little thing out of the cot and said, 'Isn't she absolutely adorable.' It was very difficult to know quite what to say. I wanted to be honest but also kind so I murmured, 'What are you going to call her?' To him she was the most beautiful little girl he had ever seen. To me she was just another little baby!

I think we have to understand that when God looks at us he is absolutely thrilled with us. In fact he is much more pleased with us than we are with ourselves. Remember how he said of Jesus, 'This is my beloved Son in whom I am well pleased.' Now he looks at us as he did Jesus and says, 'This is my child, and with you I am absolutely thrilled.' It is not that everything we do pleases God, because often there is disobedience and wrong things in our lives which he wants to change, but that he loves us because we are his children.

Secondly, a father loves his children for who they are. I overheard a mother recently saying to her child, 'Mummy doesn't love little girls who do that sort of thing.' I do hope that what she meant was she didn't like her little girl misbehaving, but it wouldn't alter the fact that she loved her whatever she did. My love for my children does not depend upon what they do. I like them to be well behaved, but my love for them is not diminished by their behaviour.

Let me underline some basic truths:

1. Our salvation is a gift. We receive it solely because of God's grace.
2. Grace is the undeserved favour of God towards us.
3. We can do nothing at all to earn God's acceptance.
4. As Christians we can still do nothing to earn acceptance from him.
5. He loves us because we are his children.
6. We obey him because we love him, not to earn anything from him.

Remember—Grace + anything = law. We are no longer under law. It's grace + nothing!

Thirdly, a father finds that he shares his children's joys. I have often found myself looking out of the window to notice the children really enjoying themselves, laughing and playing together in the garden. Most normal children, of course, tend to intersperse times of happiness with punching each other's heads in! But in spite of those interludes it is easy to get caught up in their times of joy. So too is God involved with our happiness. Psalm 149:4 says, 'For the Lord takes pleasure in his people.'

I don't know how often we have thought of God looking down on us with big, warm smiles of enjoyment. If my children were to ask me what it is that makes me enjoy them, they might say, 'Why is it that I give you such pleasure? Is it because of my good looks, or because of my ability, or because of my good behaviour?' My answer of course would be, 'No, it is none of those things. It is because you are my child.' My approval, love and joy in my children is not related to ability, but to the fact that they are my children.

It is important for us to grasp the difference between God's acceptance of us and his desires for us. That is why the kingdom of God is so closely related to understanding God's fatherhood. When we become Christians it is because we desire to put ourselves under the lordship of Christ. Therefore his desire for us is that we are obedient and do the things that he asks us to do. But his love for us is not based upon what we do but on who we are. And we are what we are because of Christ and not our good deeds. His acceptance of us is first and foremost because of what Christ has done for us. God can only accept us because Christ died for us and now we are in Christ. There is nothing we can do that will ever give us God's acceptance. In fact Paul makes it quite clear that even our own righteousness is like filthy rags. As far as God is concerned even the good things we have done are filthy, in that they come short of perfection and are therefore inadequate.

Paul goes to great lengths to underline again and again in the epistles that the gospel we have received is a gospel of grace, and that we can do nothing of ourselves to make ourselves acceptable to God. It is a gift from God. That is what grace is all about. It is receiving the undeserved favour of God. But Paul goes on to ask the question, 'Are we to continue in sin that grace may abound? By no means! How can we who died to sin still live in it?' (Romans 6:1–2). Although grace is freely given we are to live in obedience. Jesus said, 'If you love me keep my commandments.' His love for us is not conditional upon what sort of people we are, but purely because we have become his children. When we come to a place where we know that because of Christ's death on the cross we are forgiven, we put our lives into the hands of God, becoming subjects in his kingdom, receiving the Spirit, experiencing and knowing the love of God on a day-to-day basis. Then and only then have we come into real freedom. And Paul says, 'For freedom Christ has set us free' (Galatians 5:1). In other words not only has Christ set us free, but we are intended to live in that tremendous freedom day by day.

We are saved by God's grace, and there will be evidence of our having received that grace in the way we live. Our lives will be changed and we will have a desire to obey and serve the Lord if his grace has really begun its work in us. We are not saved by works, but works will follow real faith and love.

A father also shares the pain of his children. I have heard many parents say that sometimes they find themselves caught up in their children's emotions if they come home from school unhappy, or they don't want to go to school for some reason or other. In other words, they identify with their children. I can think of many occasions when I would rather have gone to school and sat in the classroom than let my children go! I suppose that is because it evokes all the same reactions that I had as a child, and because they are part of me, I find myself entering into their feelings quite deeply. One of my boys might come back from school one day and tell me that some other child has been nasty to him. I know my reaction sometimes is that I would like to go and pick up that other child and beat him across the playground (in love of course!). Do you ever feel like that? Sometimes you hear the teacher has been a bit unkind. Your reaction is to want to defend your child and be aggressive towards the teacher.

Now, because children's pain is felt by their parents it doesn't mean to say that a responsible parent takes his children out of the difficult situation. Children have to learn and they have to grow up. Part of that growing-up process is to go through the difficult things of life. In exactly the same way, God shares our pain because of his love and commitment to us. God is intrinsically caught up with our situation, not because of emotional weakness that makes him very susceptible to our fears and problems, but because he is a father and understands. That is why to be a parent can fill you with tremendous joy and tremendous pain if you are really expressing love towards your children.

No wonder the prophets, when they wrote, expressed so much of the feelings of God. You only have to read some of their writings, particularly the minor prophets, to know that God was deeply and totally involved with his people. He was so filled with joy when they were obedient and followed him, and so full of pain when they disobeyed. You don't sense in any way that God is removed and distant from his people, or that he makes purely objective statements about them. Here is a God who feels deeply and is involved with his people. His love never changes towards them. But he is also a God who doesn't allow his emotions to rule him. He is obviously totally in control of each and every situation. He decides what he is going to do. I know that I can very easily behave erratically and lose control of a situation, but God is never like that. He is not swayed by a momentary emotional feeling, but is utterly in control of everything he does and says. This universe is his and it is held in his hands. It is an incredible thing to understand that in every joy and pain of life, every act of suffering, every difficult situation, our God not only knows what we are going through, but he actually feels it. In Exodus 3:7 it says: 'Then the Lord said, "I have seen the affliction of my people who are in Egypt, and have heard their cry because of their task masters; I know their sufferings, and I have come down to deliver them out of the hand of the Egyptians."'

How many times have you heard a child say, 'Dad, why do I have to go to school?' or, 'If only I didn't have to do this or that life would be great!' How many times have you said, 'God, if you are there, get me out of this situation!' or, 'If God really loved me he wouldn't allow me to go through this!' A father who really loves his children allows them to go through situations which are difficult but are not going to harm them. A human father is actually more concerned about the protection of his children than his children are for their own safety; it's just that a good father has a better idea of what constitutes 'protection'.

You may have noticed that when you take your children out, or go across the road, it is usually you who takes the initiative to say, 'Come and hold my hand.' It is not that you are particularly nervous, or that you have never crossed the road before, but you are concerned about your children! You only have to be in a busy shopping area on a Saturday to hear mums screaming at their children to stay with them and hold their hands, or issuing other unprintable instructions concerning their protection! Children very rarely want to hold anybody's hand to cross the road—after all a seven-year-old knows everything about life! But parents have a bigger vision and a greater understanding of danger and they are the ones who reach down and hold their children's hand. A good father is more concerned about the welfare of his children than the children are for themselves.

The parent is the one who is concerned about their education, their future, what they do with their time. They are concerned for their happiness, their fulfilment and that they make the most of their gifts and talents.

These are the things that concern a human father. How much more do they concern the heavenly Father who is longing to see us fulfilled and making the most use of the gifts and talents he has given us. After all, when he made the world he saw that it was good, and he put us in it to enjoy fully all that he had made. So his concerns for us are really for our welfare and for our good.

God is supremely concerned about us and our needs. He is more concerned about our lives than we are. We all know how concerned we are about our own lives! It is amazing to know that God is more concerned. He watches us every minute. He sees every action. He knows every thought. And his plans are for our good. He is the One who is protecting us and he is the One who safeguards our lives.

Many people often say. 'If God is a God of love he wouldn't allow this or that to happen.' If we approach God in that way then we will find our lives to be a continual see-saw. One day we will be impressed with the love of God because things are going well; the next day, because things are difficult, we will wonder whether there is a God of love. To start a sentence with the word 'if' will always prove destructive in our lives. As Christians we take the word of God as truth, as a foundation to everything else. His word, revealed in the Bible, clearly states that God is a father who loves, therefore we can say, '*Because* God is a God of love, what is happening to me is a part of his tender care and concern.' (Even if I am under enemy attack and learning how to fight.)

It is the parents' responsibility to provide for their children. I don't ask my children to provide food, clothing and shelter. These are not their problems and they don't have to be concerned about that sort of thing. It is my responsibility, and I provide all the necessary things of life for them. I am more concerned that they have these things than they are. This is something of the tremendous truth Jesus was teaching in Matthew 6. As a friend of mine often says, 'If you don't believe that God loves you like this then you are saying that he is more concerned about his garden and his pets than he is about his children.'

We will look at Matthew 6 a little later on, but basically the teaching is that God is the One who is concerned about our provision. God is the One who is concerned about our shelter. He will provide all these things for us. Why? Because he is a father. He doesn't do that for all mankind, but he *will* do it for those who have submitted themselves and become his children. This is not referring to the quantity of the resources we have, but it is a promise to provide the necessities of life.

Jesus came from his throne in heaven to tell us that God's attitude towards us is one of a father for his children. He went on to say that even though the human attitude of a father towards his child gives us some understanding of this we all harbour evil and selfish hearts and therefore our love towards our own children is grossly inadequate. If we in our humanity can begin to understand the powerful feelings of a father towards a child, how much greater, how much deeper, how much more extensive, how much more embracing, is the love of God towards you and me. It is a love which is not just something that is general to everybody, but is a love that is specific to every man, woman and child who has become a child of God.

Of course, it is true that God loves all men and he longs for every man to be saved (1 Timothy 2:3–4), but there is a special father/child love that comes into being when a person responds to him. He reaches out to all men because he wants them to be able to share in these privileges.

The great cry which wells up from our hearts time and time again is: 'But not me!' The writer of the Hebrews makes it quite clear that God intends us to come into a place of rest in our hearts. It isn't a place of inactivity but a place of peace. He compares it with the children of Israel entering the promised land. He says that the main reason they didn't enter was their unbelief. This unbelief resulted in hardened hearts. It is very easy to allow unbelief to enter in and then we become hard and cynical towards God. The place of peace is to know God's love and care for us, and to understand that we are being held in his arms. He never removes us from the difficulties and trials of this world in which we live, but in it all Jesus is Emmanuel, God with us. He is with us! The psalmist wrote: 'Yea, though I walk through the valley of the shadow of death, I will fear no evil: for thou art with me; thy rod and thy staff they comfort me' (Psalm 23:4, AV). It isn't that God removes us from the difficult experiences of life, but rather that he shares them with us and becomes our strength in the midst of them. This glorious fact enables us not only to conquer but to be more than conquerors!

4

The Child's Response

'Why have you got such a big nose?' That was the opening question of a three-year-old whose family I visited recently. It was the first time I had been to their home and I didn't know the family well. 'To keep my glasses on my face,' was the only reply that I felt would satisfy him.

Some children have a wonderful way of being open and honest, and able to express what they really feel! Somehow they bypass and override all the protocol and etiquette that we have applied to our adult lives. There is also a sort of carefreeness about children. If you ever watch them in a playground you will notice, interspersed with the crying and quarrelling, that they run around together laughing, shouting and skipping. There is an eagerness and an excitement about even the smallest thing. How often have you looked at a group of small children and thought how nice it would be to be young again? Not that any of us would want to go back to school, but it just seems that when we become adults we take on so many cares, worries and anxieties. Children seem to be so free of them.

It seems that when we attain adulthood we have to take on so many worries and concerns as well. Of course we have to become responsible, and increased responsibility is one of the attributes of growing up, but that doesn't mean we have to be bowed down with care and worry. No wonder Jesus said that to enter the kingdom we need to become like little children. It is so easy to look at them and think how good it would be to have that carefree attitude to life, to be able to skip and jump. Well, we can. Children have a direct sort of approach to life. They are not terribly concerned with the past and they have very little concern for the future. Their lives are lived for the moment and they are primarily interested in what is happening to them now. Of course children do have cares, but they are usually about small things that have to do with the immediate situation. Usually, to the adult, they seem so insignificant and trivial. That is because the adult has a wider perspective on life.

Wouldn't it be strange if I came down to breakfast one morning to see my nine- and eleven-year-old children looking worried and distraught, with furrowed brows, and on enquiring what the trouble was they replied: 'Dad, neither of us were able to sleep properly last night because we were so worried. We are concerned that you and Mum are unable to cope with this rate increase we saw on the news last night. We are concerned too about your tax returns for last year. We have been worried about our education and whether you have got it all mapped out for the future. Then there are all the problems of Mum and the housekeeping and whether we are going to have enough food for the next week or so.' I would think there was something very wrong with my children if they began to behave in that sort of way. All those things are my responsibility.

Of course, in a family it is important that everyone shares the things that are happening to them so that everybody feels involved, but the sense of responsibility rests with the parents and not the children.

Children just assume that these things will be provided. They realize they won't have everything they want, but assume they will have what they need. This assumption is based on the relationship they have with us and the realization that we care about them and that we are responsible for looking after them—as well as the fact that living in the West we are able to provide material things for them. Of course the degree of security differs from family to family. It is not related to wealth but to personal relationships. Many poor children are more secure than rich ones because they know they are loved, even if they don't have an abundance of material things. This provision is of course dependent on the parents' ability to obtain food, etc. In the Third World today, children go without because there are just not the resources available, and the tragedy we are all aware of takes place.

I need to mention here that there might be times, on account of certain circumstances and situations, where we don't have a permanent dwelling place and where the normal provisions of life are not available. However, because of the relationship they have with their parents those children still have a sense of security.

You see, nothing is ours by right. There is a great temptation to believe that we have a right to certain privileges in life. We then find that our lives are a continual struggle to achieve, and to attain what we believe we are entitled to. There is a very real sense in which we as Christians have no rights. Everything is a gift from God. It would be dangerous to think that because God is my Father I am therefore entitled to this that or the other. What it means is this: because God is my Father I can assume that he is providing basic needs for me at any given time. Paul said that he had learnt to be abased and to abound. He also said, 'I have learned, in whatever state I am, to be content' (Philippians 4:11). Paul talks here of knowing he has sufficient and it is that attitude that God desires for us—where all sense of anxiety and fear goes because in the midst of anything that is happening to us we know that we are in the hands of God.

When Jesus wrote in Matthew 6:25, 'Do not be anxious . . .' his reasoning was that 'the Father knows what you need'. In other words, if we really understand and grasp that God has a father's heart towards us and that we are his children then these issues, i.e. food, clothing and shelter which represent the basic needs of life, are God's responsibility towards us.

Most of our anxieties concern the future. We are anxious that there may not be adequate material provision. We are anxious about our safety. We are anxious about the direction of our lives. We become anxious about a multitude of possibilities, but usually these things never actually come to fruition. Our hearts have been needlessly filled with anxiety about them. Jesus was quite clear in stating that this attitude towards life is sinful, because it is rooted in unbelief.

There is a story told of Martin Luther who, on finding a farmer sitting by the roadside looking as if the troubles of the whole world had suddenly fallen on his shoulders, asked him: 'Why do you look so depressed?'

'Well, last night there was a fire on my farm. It not only destroyed my house but it also burned down my barns filled to the roof with the best crop of wheat I have ever had.'

'Do you know the Apostles' Creed?' questioned the reformer.

'Of course I do,' huffed the farmer.

'Then say it,' replied Martin Luther.

'I believe in God. . . .'

'Stop! Say it louder,' said Luther.

'I believe in God. . . .'

'Louder still and with much more conviction,' insisted Luther.

'*I believe in God the Father*. . .' declared the farmer at the top of his voice.

Martin Luther then said that if the farmer really believed that the almighty God was his Father, then even if he lost 100 farms it could not possibly make any difference because such a God could easily provide him with 1000 more!

When Jesus gave this amazing teaching he was not condemning forward planning or preparation, nor was he saying that material things are unimportant. He was forbidding worry. Satan continually wants to get our minds either on material things so they become our treasure, or on worry. God's desire is that we set our minds on Christ. The battle is a battle for the mind. What happens in our minds affects the way we behave, the things we talk about, and very often our physical health. This passage in Matthew 6 underlines certain things about worry.

Blind

Worry is blind. It denies the obvious revelation of the world around us. It is true that God gives life. Therefore he will surely sustain it. It is true that God made the body. So he will surely clothe it. He reminded the disciples that, as they looked around the world about them, both the birds of the air and the lilies of the field were provided for. If we look carefully we will see that God has abundantly provided for things in the natural world. How much more will he provide for us. (Note that he is in no way saying we shouldn't think seriously about life, nor is he saying we shouldn't work.)

Jesus told his disciples to look at the birds of the air. As we look at them we find they are provided with food. They don't create it, but it is available to them. We are the ones who work, but God is the One who provides. He is the source of all we have. It is interesting to notice that Jesus said: '*Your* heavenly Father feeds them.' The same heavenly Father who feeds the birds feeds us. Then Jesus asked the question: 'Are you not of more value than they?'

Then he asks us to consider, meditate on, or think about the lilies of the field. In other words he isn't just asking us to glance at them. If we stop to think about our surroundings we are struck by the beauty of nature. It is obvious that the flowers and the trees don't toil and sweat; so where did their beauty come from? It is a gift from God. Then doesn't this make sense: 'Will he not much more clothe you?' Beauty comes to those whose hearts are at peace because they trust the Lord to sustain them.

Faithless

Worry is faithless. When Jesus said: 'O you of little faith,' he was talking to his disciples. Why is worry faithless? It is faithless because it denies firstly that God is interested in us, secondly that he wants to help us, and thirdly that he is powerful enough to do anything about it. All of us who have become Christians have done so by faith. We have faith in the effectiveness of Christ's death on the cross. We trust in him and believe that our sins are forgiven because he died for us. We receive the Holy Spirit by faith into our lives. We haven't seen him or touched him but we ask him to enter in by faith, that is, by trust. The writer to the Hebrews reminds us that: 'Without faith it is impossible to please him' (Hebrews

11:6). In other words it is possible to be a Christian and yet at the same time exercise very little faith and therefore fail to please God.

Faith is belief in action. It is easy to live a life that is like anybody else's except that we attend church and Bible study groups, and add Bible reading and prayer to our list of activities. Our lives are intended to be lived in such a way that as others look at us they can see we are really trusting God. In other words if God wasn't there our lives would fall apart. Worry is a denial of faith. How can we say we have faith and trust God yet at the same time be anxious? Anxiety expresses unbelief, therefore it is sin.

Jesus said that the Gentiles, i.e. unbelievers or those who are not Christians, should be the ones to worry. And so they should. If there is no God and we have no relationship with him then there is an enormous amount to worry about. Jesus was saying that they didn't know, believe or experience God, so no wonder they worried. But we are not to behave like those non-Christians. Isn't it marvellous to read those words of Jesus: 'The Father knows.' He knows our needs, he knows our situation, he knows our past and he knows our future.

It is interesting to note here that he relates the whole concept of fatherhood to seeking the kingdom of God. In other words the way to discover this peace with God and the reality of the fatherhood of God is actually to seek first the kingdom of God and his righteousness. That means wanting to see Jesus as King and Lord in every area of our lives and also to desire to be holy. If (first and foremost) we want Jesus to be the boss—for our lives to be lived in obedience to him, and to please him—then we will discover the peace of knowing that God is a caring father. These two concepts are directly related.

Futile

Jesus said that worry is futile. It is pointless as it cannot change the past, and the future is uncertain anyway. It is probably true to say that our most major worries concern things that never happen. How much time is wasted and how much effort is given to worrying about the future? We then discover that the reality is never what it appeared to be. After all, being anxious about a situation never changed it anyway. All that happens is that our hearts become heavy, weary and bowed down. It is utterly futile to be anxious because it doesn't make the slightest bit of difference.

It is amazing how many of our lives are lived either in the past or the future. It is so easy to look back to the past, either with rosy-coloured spectacles and think of the good old days and all the apparently wonderful things that happened, or with regret and live on the basis of 'if only . . .'. So many of us are saying: 'If only I had got this, if only I hadn't done that,' and we are living condemned by the past. If we are haunted by the past it will destroy the present. Praise God that even if we have done wrong and made mistakes Jesus washes the past clean and we can start again. The wonderful thing is that we can live again in the present knowledge that the past is dealt with.

The other temptation is to live in the future—dread of the future characterized by the words 'but what if . . .', or fantasy about the future summed up by: 'When this happens everything will be all right.' In reality none of us live in the past and none of us live in the future, but we all live in the present. If God is sufficient for our needs today then he must be sufficient for our needs tomorrow.

When the children of Israel were provided with miraculous food in the wilderness they had to learn a very great lesson about God's provision. God provided the manna every day. Each time they had to believe that the manna would be there again the next day. (Except of course for one day when they had to collect twice as much because there was to be no provision on the Sabbath.) Now some of them were tempted to hang on to what they had in case none came the following day. When that happened what they had went sour and mouldy. When God provides for us, and we are thrilled with his provision, it is very easy to believe that there won't be any more coming in the future. When that happens we tend to hang on to what we have got and it so easily turns sour on us. God's provision is for today, and tomorrow's provision will come tomorrow.

I don't need to be concerned about tomorrow because I am living today. Either God is a father who cares intimately about the needs of his children, and therefore our security is utterly dependable, or God is not what the Bible says he is. We need to decide where the truth lies and live accordingly. The clear teaching of the New Testament, brought primarily through Jesus, is that God is the Father and Provider.

We either live out our lives in the belief that this is true or we don't.

Harmful

It is important to notice that worry is harmful. Many times we hear medical reports to the effect that worry is the cause of many serious physical disorders. It wears a person out physically and mentally and is an utterly destructive force in our lives. There is nothing to be gained by worry and everything to be lost.

Jesus calls us to live a day at a time. He is the One who knows the future. Of course we are to plan and to be prepared but we are not to fear. Isn't it wonderful to hear the psalmist—who went through all sorts of hardship and difficulty in his life as well as great times of victory and joy—saying: 'I have been young, and now am old; yet I have not seen the righteous forsaken or his children begging bread' (Psalm 37:25).

It is a good exercise to examine our thoughts when we lie awake at night, or when we walk down the street, or at other times when they are not being fixed on some particular matter. It is then we begin to realize what we are anxious about. Those are the thoughts that come back to our minds time and again.

How desperately we need to take those thoughts and put them alongside the truth that God is a father, and see how they look in the perspective of that reality.

Let us link this chapter to the next with these words from the prophet Habakkuk:

> Though the fig tree do not blossom,
> nor fruit be on the vines,
> the produce of the olive fail
> and the fields yield no food.
> the flock be cut off from the fold
> and there be no herd in the stalls,
> yet I will rejoice in the Lord,
> I will joy in the God of my salvation.
> God, the Lord, is my strength;
> he makes my feet like hinds' feet,
> he makes me tread upon my high places.
>
> (Habakkuk 3:17–19)

5

A Father Who Restores

Nina

Nina was a very attractive twenty-five-year-old Asian girl who at the age of eighteen had come over to England to study. This was the first time she had been outside her own country, so it was a time of discovering all sorts of new experiences and meeting a wide variety of people that she had never come into contact with before. It was during her time at college that she had become friendly with some girls who were committed Christians. Through sharing with them and watching them she had seen her own need for Jesus and had given her life to him.

She experienced a tremendous change in herself and her outlook on life, but the time came for her to finish college and she felt that she would like to further her understanding of her Christian faith. So she went to Bible college. It was while she was there that she again heard the message that God is a father who loves and cares for his children. She was sure in her mind that she had become a child of God when she had given her life to Christ, but somehow the message always caused a negative reaction in her spirit. She found herself wanting to run away and not listen to what was being said. Something stirred deep within her.

As a small child she had been brought up in a large family and her father, who was obviously a disturbed man, had violently beaten both her and her mother on many occasions. There had been a break when he walked out on the family and was not seen for nearly a year. She remembered that it had been such a quiet, restful time in their home. Then the news came that her father had returned, was repentant and wanted to be reunited with his family. Although her mother was overjoyed, she found that it filled her own heart with fear to have him back in the home. It wasn't long after this that the beating started again. Her only memory of her father was the angry and vicious way he looked at her and treated her.

When she came to England she found a whole new way of living. She made new friends who cared for her and accepted her. On top of this her Christian faith had given her a new confidence again. But somehow she was never really able to trust God and couldn't ultimately believe that he cared for her specifically.

James

James, too, found it difficult to grasp any understanding of God's love for him. He had become a Christian after examining the facts and evidence for the life, death and resurrection of Jesus. He was intellectually convinced of the truth and therefore realized that he needed to respond to it in some way, but he had never really allowed the gospel message to touch him emotionally. Although he came from a fairly wealthy home and relatively happy childhood, his father who had been very close to him, had walked out on his mother when he was nine years old and he had only seen him on odd occasions since then. He always bought him expensive presents and gifts, but they were a poor substitute for what he really wanted. He didn't really like to talk about his father because it brought to the surface all sorts of things he would rather stifle.

Jane

Jane was slightly different. She had had a good upbringing and a happy childhood. She was in her late twenties and single. Although she had been a Christian for many years she had never really been able to trust God—in fact she felt she couldn't trust anybody. At the age of eighteen she had fallen deeply in love with a boy and established a very close relationship with him. They had made a commitment that by the time she was twenty-two they would be married. She really had given everything to this relationship and had waited with great expectancy for their wedding day. It was only a few days before the actual wedding when he announced that he wanted to cancel his engagement to her. He made it clear that he had in fact met someone else some weeks before and he realized he couldn't go ahead with both of them. In the intervening six years she had not been able to have any close relationships, certainly not with men. There was a lot of hurting and a lot of pain still there.

Ann

'My trouble is that I can't be trusted to do anything. I am one of those people who always fails!' So spoke Ann. She went on to share that she knew God couldn't trust her and that she had never really been any use to him. She too looked back on her childhood. She had been the eldest of three children. She remembered how much her parents had loved her and cared for her until about the age of six or seven when her younger sister was born. From then on it seemed as if she was the only person who really mattered and Ann felt totally discarded. All the time she was compared to her younger sister and told how wonderful her newborn sister was and this went on into teenage years. It seemed that she was always the one who did things wrong. She could still remember the continual cry of her mother: 'You never do anything right. You ought to be more like your sister. If only you could be trusted like she can....'

These people had all been together in the same room. There were several hundred others too, and I wondered how many more were hurting inside. But these people, and there are thousands upon thousands like them, all have something in common and that is that they have been hurt at some stage in their lives by the sin of others. The great tragedy is that the damage caused is not primarily due to the initial sin but their reaction to it. Apparently there is a certain sort of snake that when cornered and very angry will bite itself. This is what happens to us when we react to circumstances in our lives—we end up being the ones that are damaged.

Respond or react

When someone sins against us we can either respond to it in forgiveness, and release that person from the hurt they caused us, or we can react. In our vulnerability, particularly in early life when we have our only real security in our family, we are very easily hurt by other people. If the family is secure we find it much easier to respond positively to the hurts in the world around us because we know we have some secure, loving relationships. When the source of that hurt comes from our own family there is often only one thing we can do and that is to react in some self-protective way. It produces bitterness and anger and often a deep sense of rejection.

Once that attitude is firmly rooted in us, even subconsciously, then the patterns repeat themselves again and again. We find that in the difficult situations of life we react to them instead of responding. Reaction is caused because of previous experiences. We respond to situations only when we are free.

When we come to Christ and experience his forgiveness and new life, we do become his children. The trouble is that all too often we bring our bad reactions with us into our Christian experience and from then on we find it difficult to understand why we behave the way we do. We find ourselves reacting in exactly the same way as we have done for years, even towards the love of God.

Repentance

When Jesus talked about repentance as a necessary part of entering into the kingdom of God, he was referring to the need to turn away from all past sin and follow him. As we have seen, when Jesus began his ministry he went through the waters of baptism, not for his own sin but as a demonstration of what all of us would need to do. That is why baptism is such an important issue in the Christian life. Although the physical act of baptism is important, even more important is the baptism of our hearts. The New Testament tells us that we died with Christ, we were buried with Christ and we have risen with Christ. Now the word 'buried' speaks of different things to different people, but here in the New Testament it refers to death. I can bury a weed deep in the garden and think that it is dealt with, but it will go on growing and coming up. For many of us we have taken the hurts and the pains and we have put them under the carpet. We say: 'Oh, that's all in the past. I've put that behind me now.' But in fact it isn't in the past at all. It's still in the present because it is buried but not dead and buried. We need to know that all our guilt, failure, lack of self-worth, hurts and pains are dead and buried—and repentance is the key.

The Bible speaks of a 'root of bitterness' that grows and develops if there is unforgiveness for past hurts. There is only one answer and that is to forgive in a very specific way. We must spell out with whom we are angry and for what. It is important to acknowledge a sense of rejection and hurt and not try to pretend it doesn't exist. Only in the safety of God's fatherly care can any of us dare to do this.

Pride is a strong enemy of repentance. It refuses to allow us to admit that we have been hurt—particularly by loved ones—and to acknowledge our wrong. The man who can confess: 'I am angry with my dad for walking out on me when I was so young. I felt he didn't care for me. Even if things were bad with Mum, why did he leave me? I love him, but I am so angry with him. Now, seeing God loves me, I forgive him from my heart'—that is a man who will know the peace and security of God. Forgiveness is an act of the will and not necessarily felt with the emotions initially. Real repentance will also result in acts of repentance—i.e. positive love.

The rejected man is always suspicious of anything that is said to him. He takes everything as either a criticism or a compliment. He needs continual reassurance. He can't believe anybody else really likes him and cannot bear to be corrected. Rejection is a reaction to hurt. The only answer is forgiveness and receiving the unreserved acceptance of God. You cannot know one without the other. No wonder that Jesus said the door into the kingdom was through repentance. The kingdom of God in our lives is the result of the Spirit of God possessing our souls. If there is bitterness, hurt and therefore resistance present, spiritual growth will always be impaired as the soul resists the intrusion of the Spirit.

Following repentance some people need deliverance from spirits of rejection and fear that have found a home in them. They will need to ask another experienced Christian to pray with them.

With each of these folk already mentioned none of them needed deep psychiatric help, or prolonged psychotherapy. As the Holy Spirit pinpointed the areas of hurt, each had to release those people who had hurt them and, as an act of repentance, forgive those who had done damage to them. It is so much easier to do this when we see that those people themselves are the victims of their own sin and satanic influence in their lives. They too are desperately in need of the love of God and have often acted quite blindly.

We don't usually need massive heart-searching sessions going back into every area of the past to see if there is anything lurking there! The Holy Spirit is very specific and accurate in his dealing with sin. If we ask him he will make it quite clear where any problems lie. That's his work.

There are too many people trapped in digging up their past, failing to live in the present reality of being new creations. But if there is sin or unforgiveness that has never been dealt with it must be sorted out.

In fact, we often find ourselves saying: 'I can't forgive her,' or, 'I can't forgive him.' There is never a time when we *can't* forgive. It is usually that we *won't* forgive. Our pride has been hurt—we have been damaged. Someone else has done something to us and we won't forgive them, so we are the ones who are hurt and spiritually crippled. Jesus tells a parable in Matthew 18:23 about a very wealthy man who was owed a large sum of money but he was prepared to forgive the debtor and let him go. But this man who had been forgiven then went out and found someone who owed him just a little and he was unable to forgive and release that man. How great was his punishment because he failed to forgive.

If we fail to forgive those who hurt us it really means that we have no understanding of the enormity of God's forgiveness towards us. We need to stop and look at the cross and to see those arms outstretched, the nails, the agony and suffering that Christ went through. Why did he do it? He did it so that we might be forgiven and accepted by God. If God has done that for us how can we not forgive those who have hurt us? But we do have a choice and we are free to choose whether or not to forgive. But we will never know the real forgiveness of God until there is forgiveness in our own hearts. Once this issue is settled and there is repentance, we know our old life is nailed to the cross, we can never again blame the past for our present behaviour. From now on we can expect 'all things to become new'. We are free to be the children of God that we were intended to be.

Sowing the seed

Jesus told a parable about receiving the word of God. He said that the word referred to the truth of the kingdom of God. In this parable, as in many of the stories of Jesus, there are different levels of understanding. The parable of the sower obviously reveals how people react to the preaching of the kingdom. We see that today, when the gospel is preached, some reject it, some receive it initially and then fall away, some last a bit longer but find their faith crushed and they give up, and others go on and there is real fruit. We can see this all around us as a response to the gospel. This gospel is the gospel of the kingdom. It has to do with the lordship of Christ in a person's life. And the reactions Jesus talked about are how people react when they hear that Jesus wants to be King in their lives. When Jesus wants to come and rule our lives it means that every area needs to submit to him. That is why Jesus was saying that not everybody will jump up and down with excitement at the message of the kingdom because repentance and change need to be the first response.

One of the major truths of the kingdom of God is that God is a father. This parable enables us to understand how we can respond to that truth and allow it to become a real day by day experience in our lives.

Jesus said that the seed was sown on different sorts of soil. The seed is the word of God which is perfect in every way. It is the soil that is different in each of these cases. The first sort of soil Jesus described as a pathway. What is a pathway? Obviously it is a place that is well worn by people walking along it and the more they walk on it the harder it becomes. All of us have well-worn paths in our lives. Our patterns of behaviour and attitudes are often protective mechanisms that are built up over the years through reactions to hurts, for example, rejection, self-pity, and resentment towards others. We see them in ourselves by the way we spontaneously react to situations, circumstances or the people that we meet in our lives.

Now the word of God comes to us that God is a father and it is possible to give mental assent to that truth without allowing it to permeate our being and become part of our lives. This is because it contradicts an attitude established over many years. It may be that those we have trusted in love relationships have hurt us, and it results in our hearts becoming hard ground. So many of us build up hard areas in our lives and fail to ever experience change, not because God's word is not true, but because we won't recognize the hardness and really desire to do something about it. That something is always repentance. That is why Jesus taught forgiveness as such a primary principle in the kingdom of God and that when we learn to forgive those who have hurt us we can open ourselves up to this seed of truth.

Prepare the soil

The prophet said, 'Break up your fallow ground, for it is the time to seek the Lord, that he may come and rain salvation upon you' (Hosea 10:12). That is a wonderful picture of breaking up hard and solid attitudes in our lives. In whatever way that ground is formed, whether it is through repeated patterns of behaviour that are contrary to the principles of the kingdom of God, or attitudes towards people, we need to experience a turning away from that which we know is not pleasing to him. It is in the breaking up of these attitudes that release and freedom come. The beginnings of revival in our hearts are present when change or repentance is a reality.

We find as we read the Bible and hear God's word preached to us, it often contradicts the pattern of behaviour in our own lives and then we have to choose whether or not to change. We always need to be measuring ourselves up against what God says. That word only enters into our lives and is expressed in reality when there is a real change of heart. It means acknowledging that our attitudes, where they contradict the word of God, are wrong and we are the ones that must change. So much preaching is wasted because the hearers receive it, acknowledge it as true but refuse to allow it to make the slightest difference to life because it contradicts patterns already set up and there is no real intention of changing.

As Nina openly expressed her hurt and anger towards her father, released him from the responsibility of it and forgave him, it was like a dam bursting in her life. She was overwhelmed with a sense of God's love reaching right down into her innermost being, and bringing healing from the hurts and the pain of all that had gone before. She wept freely and openly. Until that time God had been unable to reach her as she put up a wall of resistance, but now there was repentance and the Spirit of God was able to enter in and deal with her at her deepest point of need.

In each of the people mentioned earlier, the real release came in their lives when there was a willingness to forgive. It wasn't necessarily easy, nor did it mean instant healing, but the process had begun and God was able to bring them into a deeper and more vital experience of his love for them.

Wise or foolish

Jesus described another sort of soil that on the surface seems good. It is the kind of soil that receives the word eagerly and the seed begins to grow very fast and appears healthy. But it is only on the surface, and it soon withers and dies because it has no root.

Jesus told another very similar parable in Matthew 7. In this he said that there are two sorts of people, both of whom have certain things in common. They both hear the word of God. They are both subject to pressures and trials in their lives. In one case the pressures caused the house (or the life) to collapse, and in the other the pressures do nothing to the firm foundation and the building that has been constructed. All of us receive pressures and difficulties in our lives, but our response to them will be dependent upon the foundation we have laid. Jesus said the wise man is the one who builds his house on the rock which has solid foundations, and the foolish man builds his house on the sand that has no foundations of any strength at all. Note that you build in times of peace not in the storm. If we don't learn the principles now it will be too late when the going gets tough.

He went on to say that these foundations are concerned not with what you say you believe but what you do with his word. It is not just a matter of hearing it, it is how you begin to apply it. In other words, to return to the previous parable, the man who grows quickly but is easily scorched by the sun (which Jesus again referred to as persecutions) is the one who has very few roots and no foundation. He is the man who gets excited by what he hears but doesn't understand the implications of it. If the word of God is really going to affect us then it has got to replace the old behaviour patterns of our lives. You see the foolish man is the one who believes and shouts loudly that God is a father who cares and loves him but has never really allowed that to affect him in the day to day attitudes and behaviour of his life. It hasn't dawned on him that this has to bring about a radical change in his lifestyle. It affects money, family, job, etc. When the real pressure comes in his life he discovers there is nothing there because he has never put his understanding of God's word to the test. Then it is too late. In the midst of difficulty all his theory goes out of the window and his life falls apart.

We must build before the storm. Unless we allow these principles to work out in our finances, in our prayer life, in evangelism, and in our families—in other words in every part of our lives—we will find that when the difficulties come all we have is mere words.

Jesus went on to say that there is a third sort of soil. This is the kind that has thorns already growing in it. This person receives the word and begins to grow and there is real repentance and change in many areas of life. There is real application of the truths and they begin to work them out. The only problem here is that alongside these truths other things are allowed to remain that are contrary to them. Jesus talked about them as the 'cares of the world', and 'the desire and deceitfulness of riches'. This is never more true than in the area of God's fatherhood. If it is true that God is our Father then these two things obviously must not be allowed to remain. Firstly, we cannot have the cares of this world and the concerns that other people have, and secondly, it must challenge our whole attitude to money.

There is only one successful way to deal with weeds and thorns and that is to pull them up at the very roots. Every time you cut them off at ground level they grow again and reappear. You can't suppress a weed! You can only kill it, and you do that by uprooting it.

The only way to deal with these major issues in our lives is to root them out at the very source. We have to decide that these elements will have to go. It means that we will have to deal drastically with the whole issue of money and worry.

The fourth type of soil is that which is described as good soil. Here there is openness and a desire at every level to change and incorporate the word of God within our lives. It means we stop putting our opinions, our views, our ideas alongside the word of God, taking in only that which is desirable to us. It means that we accept what God says as the truth and desire that for every level of our lives. We open ourselves up to it even though it costs us a great deal to do so. Of course this takes time and is part of the growing experience of the Christian life.

That is why Jesus said this seed grows, it doesn't leap or shoot up but it grows steadily. So it is with us. As we take God's word to be true as the basic principle of life and we want it to become real in us then we will grow steadily. Whenever we find that our desires and will are opposed to God's will and we obey him then that will be a growing point in our lives. This means that a decision is made to accept God's will when it is in conflict with ours, and to embrace it wholeheartedly.

Jesus is described as 'the Word become flesh'. In other words, the will of God was fully expressed in his life. It is God's desire that our lives perfectly express his will. That is what holiness is all about, and the key to it is dealing with the soil of our hearts. Where his will crosses our will, if we take his we will be on the road to holiness. The exciting truth is that God's will for us is good.

6

A Father Who Provides

Some years ago some friends of friends loaned us their house in Morecombe for four days to give us a break with the children. As we approached the town we realized that we had left behind all our money, and the cheque book too! It suddenly seemed a bit crazy to be coming away for a four-day break in someone else's house and not having any money. But God seemed to give us peace and in the car we prayed that somehow he would provide for our needs during those few days.

We knew that the house owners would be away and there would be no obvious provision for us during that time. When we arrived and opened the front door, we found an envelope on the table in the living room, and in it quite a large amount of cash. The note attached indicated that it was for our use! It was just what we needed to provide food and entertainment during those few days. The Lord had already gone ahead of us and showed us that he really is the provider.

Early on in our marriage, as we started out trusting the Lord together, we found that he often provided amounts of money that specifically equalled a particular need, in order to encourage us that it was his hand providing. Our very first telephone bill was accompanied by another envelope containing the exact amount of money with which to pay the bill! As this happened on a number of occasions it was a tremendous encouragement because it showed us the truth of God's promise that he would be our provider. But we didn't go on getting cheques that matched bills because God doesn't need to do it that way every time.

Soon after this we received a wonderful gift of a car. It was a blue Hillman Imp and I remember telling everybody how it was the Lord's car and how he had provided it for us. It was some months after we had got it that I came down one morning to find a huge dent in the back left wing which had obviously been caused by someone hitting it during the night, and not bothering to stop. I was very angry and complained furiously to God about the fact that someone had hit my precious car. After a long protest, I heard that still small voice asking: 'Whose car?' After I had calmed down I found myself saying to the Lord: 'Well, it's your car . . . and it's your dent . . . and you had better pay the bill!'

We had an estimate for the repair which came to far more than we had in the bank at that time. We didn't tell anybody what the estimate was, but later that week a friend of ours was speaking at a meeting and he felt prompted to tell the people there that our car had been damaged. I am not even sure how he heard about it, but the outcome was that they took an offering which amounted to the cost of the repair—minus ten pounds. In the following few days we received two letters, each with a five pound note in it, saying that they had wanted to give us this money at the meeting but didn't have it on them. Once again the exact amount of money was provided. I am not sure that there is anything particularly special about receiving exact amounts of money, but it is certainly a good indication of God's handiwork.

Sometime after this the gear box went on the car and the garage told us the bill would be just under £200. This was quite alarming considering it was just before Christmas and we had no spare funds at the time. We put the bill on the breakfast table and told the Lord our concern about it and the next day we received a Christmas card along with a cheque for £200. When I rang the individual to thank him he told me that he had been praying and the Lord had showed him that we needed the money and he thought it was probably for our car. He was as thrilled as we were to know that he had actually been used by God in a miracle of provision.

These sorts of things are happening all the time, of course, to so many different people and it would take volumes just to recount them. To the outsider they often seem like coincidences, but when you add them up and see that they happen with a pattern and a consistency, you can see the hand of God.

The danger is that we tend to believe these amazing things only happen to people who write books! We have removed the miraculous to the category of the special Christian. God is a father to all his children and wants to be their provider. His desire is not that we should be rich but that we should prosper in all that we do, and have sufficient.

Money matters

If this teaching does not reach down as far as your wallet, it hasn't gone very deep! When Jesus taught on the fatherhood of God he implied that it would affect every area of our lives. It is bound to if the God who created this world is actually our father. It will change our whole outlook on life and probably the most significant area to be affected will be our attitude to money. The way a person treats money directly reflects their attitude towards God. Jesus makes it quite clear that our hearts will actually be where our money is. In Matthew 6:19 he says,

> Do not lay up for yourselves treasures on earth, where moth and rust consume and where thieves break in and steal, but lay up for yourselves treasure in heaven, where neither moth nor rust consumes and where thieves do not break in and steal. For where your treasure is, there will your heart be also.

In the world in which we live money represents security, status and power. In many ways it is the alternative God as it promises to provide the things that should come from a relationship with the living God. Of course, like all forms of idolatry, it starts out to be the provider and the servant and then ends up by being the master. The wonderful thing about God is that as we begin to put him in his right place as Lord then he in fact becomes our provider as well.

It is very interesting to notice the way that Paul writes to the Thessalonians and describes the change that has taken place in their lives. He doesn't just say that they had 'become Christians' but: 'How you turned to God from idols, to serve a living and true God' (1 Thessalonians 1:9). It indicates that the main change to take place when we come to Christ is a movement of our heart towards God and away from idols. John obviously thought there was a continual temptation for Christians to drift back into idolatry when he wrote in 1 John 5:21, 'Little children, keep yourselves from idols.'

An idol is a substitute for God which enables us to remain at the centre of our own world. People worship fertility gods because they want fertility! People worship rain gods because they want rain. People centre their attentions on and offer themselves to the god that will provide them with what they need. Because all of us want security, fulfilment and identity in this world, we will look for those things that can provide them for us. It was God's original plan that as we lived out our relationship with him as Father and child, so we would find we had the ultimate security, the highest possible status and the most glorious identity. But in our sinfulness and desire to manage without God we have sought other ways to fulfil these needs.

When a person becomes a Christian he moves from idolatry to worshipping and serving the living God. This means that from then on all his provisions, security, status, and his new identity come from God the Father.

It is easy to see, though, that for many of us in our Christian lives we drift back into those forms of idolatry as we seek, for example, our security from a source other than God. It is easy to look at the Old Testament and wonder how it could have been that the children of Israel again and again turned back to idols, when they had experienced so much of God's provision and they had seen such tremendous acts of power. I so often read through those stories in the books of Joshua and Judges and wonder how they could have behaved in such a way! 'What a terrible lot they were. No wonder God had to deal with them and discipline them!' Yet exactly the same thing happens to us. We may not bow down to objects of wood or have a totem pole in the garden, but we drift back into a situation where we are looking to something or someone as our source of supply and therefore our object of worship. It is not just money either. Our work, church, and even ministry can become the centre of attention because they give us a sense of identity, well-being, etc., and therefore become idols. If we are insecure in our relationship with God then we will look to these other things and they will become central in our lives. It is easy to pin-point material objects in this way, but far more subtle and therefore more dangerous are the religious aspects of idolatry. When we doubt God's love and his power and even his existence we find we have to discover these basic needs of life elsewhere. So many of us find that we are really looking to the things of this world for our support. A great deal of what goes on in today's Christian church is a form of idolatry. It puts man and man's activity above the power of God and the worship of God.

Source of supply

There are basically two important ingredients in looking at the subject of money. First is the truth that God is the source of supply for everything we need, and secondly he expects us to be responsible with what we have.

Many of us, when asked what the source of our supply is, will say that it is our employer, or such like, because we look for the visible source of our income. Yet the truth is that God the Father is the ultimate source of everything. We often receive these resources through human means, but that is merely the way God chooses to supply our needs. He is the ultimate source.

Therefore when the means dry up (for example, we are made redundant), rather than our whole world collapsing because the source has been cut off, the truth is that it is only that particular channel which has closed, but the source of supply is as great as it ever was! God as a father will find another way to supply the same needs.

When we actually begin to grasp this truth we feel very secure because, amazing though it may seem, it means that the source of supply can never dry up. The provider can never be taken away and the heart of that provider is the heart of love. So whatever happens in the world to remove the means, or the apparent area of supply, nothing can actually change our security. No wonder this kingdom is an unshakable kingdom. The incredible thing that happens when a person becomes a Christian is that the limits of the possible become extended. We are all used to acting and behaving within the limits of what we know to be humanly possible, and within the limits of our own human and material resources. When a person is linked to God as a father the limits of those resources are the limits of God and he has no limits. In other words, anything is possible and all resources are available. No wonder Paul was able to say, 'I can do all things in him who strengthens me' (Philippians 4:13). Paul knew what it meant to have very little or to have plenty, but always he had sufficient.

This therefore means that we have to change the questions we ask. We can no longer ask: 'Is this possible?', or, 'Can we afford this?' The question becomes: 'Is this in the will and purpose of God?' Often people say they desperately need something but they just can't afford it—for example, a holiday. I think they would be surprised if they began to ask the question: 'Is it right for us to have a holiday?' If it is right, then they can begin to pray, asking God to provide. The answer may not come in terms of money, it might come in some other way, but it is an exciting adventure because they are beginning to move outside of their own resources and believe that the living God who is their Father will provide for their needs.

The next step on from this is to begin to see that God can use us to supply other people's needs particularly the poor.

Talking about holidays, a lady said to me a few days before writing this that she and her husband, who are on a very low income, had worked incredibly hard this year and were very tired. But they had no money to go away for a break. They just felt very strongly that they needed to do so and asked God to provide. They booked to go to a place in the south of England for a week or two with the children. Their main difficulty was travel as they had no money for fares. But a lady came to the house for a cup of coffee a few days before they were due to leave and as she was going out of the door, she gave them an envelope. Inside was enough money for all their rail fares, some extra spending money and a little note saying: 'This is for your holiday.' Now, she hadn't asked that person for a penny, but she *had* asked the heavenly Father, and he had asked the lady! There were two groups of people in this particular story who were responding to God in different ways.

It isn't a question of: 'I would quite like a Rolls Royce, I think I'll order one from God to arrive next week,' because what we are talking about has to do with a relationship and the basic needs of our life. In fact when you begin to know God's desires for you it changes your sense of values. For example, I know that both my boys need a bicycle. Now, if they look at their own pocket money and their own resources they know that they could never afford to go out and buy a bicycle. So I have to make an assessment as to whether this is something that is good for them to have or not. If I believe it is and I have the finances to provide for them, I can go out and buy the bicycles that they need. It would be ludicrous if I said to them: 'No, you have to live within the limits of your pocket money,' or: 'Well, you will just have to save up for the next few years in order to get the bicycle you want.' After all I would have given them the money anyway! Of course they are to be responsible with what I have given them and they are to learn to use it wisely, but there will be many occasions when they need things that are outside their own resources and they can come to me to ask for them.

So too God makes us responsible for what he gives us, but he intends us to look to him to provide over and above that. If I was excessively wealthy the question that would be uppermost in my mind would not be: 'Can I afford this?' but: 'Is it right to give it?' I don't believe that God ever scratches his head and wonders where on earth he is going to get his money from to provide for our needs. The main issue is a question of what is right for us.

Now the purpose of all this is not to make Christians rich, but to bring us into contentment and sufficiency and to be able to exercise the generosity that God wants us to express. Our prosperity is for the sake of the gospel that we can supply resources to others (2 Corinthians 9).

Jesus said, 'If you then, who are evil, know how to give good gifts to your children...' (Luke 11:13). In other words, he was expressing what is known to any father and that is that he loves to give gifts to his kids. And often he wants to give more than he knows it is wise to give. In exactly the same way Jesus said, 'How much more will the heavenly Father give the Holy Spirit to those who ask him' (Luke 11:13). God is just longing to give generously to his children. The times of hardship, as with the children of Israel, are times of God teaching us real dependence on him. We cannot afford to grow up as spoilt children but must learn to have a real dependence upon the Father and live responsibly. We must also learn to be God's means of supply to each other and particularly to the poor. We can see the failure of this on a global scale. It also has to be worked out at a local level. We still have an amazing capacity to tolerate the poverty-stricken and wealthy living alongside each other. We are called to be channels for God.

Notice Psalm 34:10, 'The young lions suffer want and hunger; but those who seek the Lord lack no good thing,' and Psalm 84:11 'For the Lord God is a sun and shield; he bestows favour and honour. No good thing does the Lord withhold from those who walk uprightly. O Lord of hosts, blessed is the man who trusts in thee!'

Living by faith

We often take the phrase 'living by faith' to describe a certain group of people who have no obvious means of financial support. These folk have felt called by God to live in this particular way and nobody actually pays them a salary. God is their direct provider. This sort of living is a particular calling. It is in fact just an extension of what all of us need to be doing, that is, seeing God as the supply, whatever the means. There have, of course, been casualties on the way. Some have started in faith, continued in hope and ended up in charity! It is certainly an exciting way to live as there is a continual reminder of God's presence and his love, but I don't think anybody would admit that it is easy. There are real hardships and although it is easy to remember the exciting stories there are always the times of testing as well.

The Bible says that all of us are to live by faith. Even though we may have a particular income every week or month, we need to see that it actually comes from the Father. Therefore it is not the limit of his provision. Of course, we must live responsibly within the bounds of what we have, but we must expect God to provide over and above that as necessary.

His real desire is for us to get to the point where we begin to look to him to supply other people's needs. I wonder if you have ever asked God to give you enough money so that you can pass it on to somebody else.

When we get to the point of seeing somebody else's need and asking God to supply us with the money in order that we can give it to them, we really have begun to live in the reality of the kingdom.

I can remember a man telling me that he and his wife believed that it was right for them to have a deep freeze, but there was no way they could afford it on his income. One day the pastor of their fellowship came to their house to pray about various things, and he agreed for the need of a deep freeze and together they looked to God to provide. When they had finished praying they decided to go down to the village to get some fish and chips. As they walked in the door of the chippy they heard the owner of the shop turn to his wife and say: 'I wonder what we should do with this deep freeze now we've bought the new one!' And he turned to this man as he walked through the door, and in the same breath continued, half jokingly, 'I don't suppose you want a deep freeze, do you?' That was a pretty quick answer to prayer.

Some friends of ours were in need of a washing machine and decided that they wouldn't ask for the money from anybody specifically but would bring the need to God. Some days later there was a knock on the door and there were two men in white coats standing on the doorstep with a large, brand new washing machine. 'We have come to deliver the washing machine,' they said. The lady in question looked at them and said, 'Well, I never ordered a washing machine, so you'll have to take it back.' The man continued, 'But we have had orders to deliver it here; it's paid for, so you had better keep it!' To this day they still do not know how the washing machine arrived at their home.

It is easy to recall the rather remarkable occurrences like that which do happen more often than we realize, but very often God provides in less spectacular yet just as real ways. Very often he will provide for us so we don't even know that it was him. It is only in retrospect that we see that it was actually an answer to our prayers.

Some friends of ours had a car that died on them and they began to pray to the Lord for a new car. The immediate answer was that they discovered friends who at that particular time were able to loan them their car for short periods. God did not immediately answer by giving them a car of their own, but he provided for their needs. God's requirement of us is that we use responsibly what we have but at the same time expect him to provide over and above that as needs arise. What an exciting adventure God has called us to!

Now some will say: 'There is something very trivial about talking of God in terms of washing machines and cars when the real needs of this world are far greater and deeper.' One of the major issues in our world is poverty. The tremendous distress that is being caused to so many in the world is of course in a different category from most of our daily petty needs. If we only live at this small minded, personal-need orientated level then we will fail to enter into God's real desire for us. But with my own children, in addition to being concerned about major issues of education and their future welfare, I am also concerned about smaller 'problems' like finding a small marble that has rolled under the bed! I care about their bicycles breaking down, *and* the future direction of their lives. I am a father and I don't judge things just by large and small. I don't say that because I am concerned with large and important issues that I don't therefore have any time to be involved with the small things of their life. God is concerned with major global issues and he is also concerned with the minute things of our daily living.

Giving

One of the reasons many of us find it difficult and are struggling financially is that we haven't grasped the very basic principles that God has laid down with regard to money. The most fundamental of these is that we are all called to be givers. Most of us find it terribly hard to give because we only just have enough to survive on ourselves. But in fact it isn't a question of amount, it has to do with sacrifice. It is easy to talk about money, but it is when we actually come to give it away, which is the real act of faith, that we discover how much we value its security. It is amazing that even though we have seen God provide again and again, any spare money we have is very difficult to part with. There is always the feeling that God might not provide again!

The issue really is not of reckless giving but of obedient giving. When we do give, what we are actually saying is that we trust God will provide for us. We have to be vulnerable in order to prove that.

Now many have debated whether tithing should be a principle for us today. This is not the place to discuss that at any length except to say that it definitely was an Old Testament principle. It did not begin with Moses and the Law but was the practice of Abraham. Surely in the New Testament, in the era of grace, it is no longer just a question of giving a tenth but of giving all. We should be giving far more under the new covenant. Therefore if tithing is an Old Testament principle then the New Testament one is that we will give at least that. If tithing helps us to be disciplined, and most of us need discipline in giving, then it is certainly a good basis to start from. If we're honest, many who don't believe in tithing (because they see it purely as belonging to the Old Testament), in reality give less than a tenth. Very often people who fight against tithing are actually not giving much at all and they use this as an excuse. The enthusiastic giver is happy to tithe—as a starting point. Of course, it costs a poor man much more to give 10% than a rich man, even if the sum is not as great. The danger of tithing is if it becomes legalistic and we never progress beyond it into 'free will offering'.

What happens for most of us is that we ask God to provide more for us and when he does we increase our standards of living so that there is less to give away. If we can decide what our basic level of living should be then we can be free to give beyond it.

The promise of Scripture is that if we give, God will give to us. That doesn't mean that our motive for giving should be in order to receive, but it is a principle that as we give God will give back to us in greater measure. It is also a principle in the Christian life that what we sow we will also reap, and if we sow generously we will reap generously. If we are mean in our giving we will also be hard up. The basic principles of sowing are that we reap later than we sow and we reap more than we sow, but it is also true that the yield will depend on where we sow. Haphazard giving does not guarantee return. Obedient giving does.

It would seem that as God sees an open channel for the flow of finances, he will bless those sort of people because he knows that the money won't get stuck. There are large sums of money in the Christian church. Money is no problem except that it has got stuck in the pockets of Christians.

Jesus said, 'Give, and it will be given to you; good measure, pressed down, shaken together, running over' (Luke 6:38).

A friend of ours, an ordinary housewife, was at a meeting recently during which there was an offering taken. On this occasion she was really challenged over the whole issue of giving. It seemed that God had taken that particular moment to speak to her on this matter. That morning she had been to the bank and drawn out her housekeeping for the week which was usually sufficient for her to get through, but rarely did she have anything over. She felt God was prompting her to put a quarter of her housekeeping into the offering. Now this was a very big step for her and a terrific challenge, but she went ahead and at the end of the week was tremendously excited, saying that not only had she got through the week, but she seemed to have a lot of money left over which was quite unusual. She had begun to experience the biblical principle of giving. God has an amazing ability to enable a little to go a long way. The principle of 2 Corinthians 8:15—'He that gathered much did not have too much, and he that gathered little did not have too little' (NIV), seems to always hold true.

In 2 Kings 4 we read of the widow and the cruse of oil. She only discovered the magnitude of supply as she poured out the oil. The miracle took place as she began to pour. God's miracle of provision takes place for us as we learn to give. Only as we give do we discover the faithfulness of his provision.

Where are we to give?

The Bible gives two main indications, although there are almost certainly others. The first is that we should give to the poor. Although here in our Western culture we don't have deprivation and malnutrition on the same scale as in the undeveloped world, there are many people who are living financially inadequate lives. We tend to assume that the Welfare State will take care of all their needs, but it is blatantly obvious that this is not the case. All around us are people who are living in very real poverty, particularly in the inner city. Is there really any reason why money from wealthier middle-class sectors should not be poured into inner-city homes? So much of our money in the suburban areas of the city goes to propping up buildings instead of being used for the needs of people. This is the great drawback of church buildings. They are a tremendous drain on resources when money could well be spent on people.

Secondly, the New Testament speaks of giving to those who are in full-time Christian work. The Bible makes it clear that the labourer is worthy of his hire. In the past we have always paid people in ministry an inadequate amount. We have allowed their living standards to be below the average member of the church. The old dictum: 'Lord, if you keep him humble we'll keep him poor,' has been close to reality. What they do with what they are given is up to them, but we do have a responsibility to honour those who minister to us.

Some people say: 'Well, I can't afford to give.' The answer to that is we can't afford not to give. If the New Testament principle is that as we give we shall receive, then the only way to receive God's provision for us is to start to give to others. This giving will be financial, but that will not be our only form of giving. This giving should not be out of guilt, or out of a feeling that we ought to do so, but out of obedience to God's clear word to us that this is how we should live. No wonder Paul said that God loves a hilarious giver.

'Your Father knows what you need,' means that it is God's responsibility to provide for our needs. Our responsibility is to give and be aware that we may well be the channel to provide for the needs of others.

We have to seriously ask ourselves whether we have ever really given sacrificially. Have we ever done anything that left us vulnerable and needing God to step in? Have we begun to live dangerously in the area of giving? Notice Paul's words in 2 Corinthians 8:1–5, 14–15:

> We want you to know, brethren, about the grace of God which has been shown in the churches of Macedonia, for in a severe test of affliction, their abundance of joy and their extreme poverty have overflowed in a wealth of liberality on their part. For they gave according to their means, as I can testify, and beyond their means, of their own free will, begging us earnestly for the favour of taking part in the relief of the saints—and this, not as we expected, but first they gave themselves to the Lord and to us by the will of God... Your abundance at the present time should supply their want, so that their abundance may supply your want, that there may be equality. As it is written, 'He who gathered much had nothing over, and he who gathered little had no lack.'

7

A Father Who Speaks

Not long ago I saw this newspaper cutting:

> TAIPEH. Tuesday. The persistence of a young Formosan who wrote 700 love letters to his girlfriend proposing marriage has brought results—she is to marry the postman who delivered them!

Spending time with Jesus will lead us to fall in love with him. Falling in love with him will mean we want to spend more time with him.

If I were to head this chapter 'prayer', I am sure a large number of people would skip over it because so often prayer is presented as a religious duty which we find hard and taxing. It easily becomes a pressure when people tell us we ought to pray. It is noticeable that books on prayer don't sell in great numbers.

When Jesus talked about prayer, though, he wasn't talking about a religious activity but about a relationship. All that the people of his day knew about prayer was what they observed in the Pharisees. They saw it as an activity that you had to endure and work hard at, certainly not enjoy. But then Jesus entered the scene and he was totally different.

There is only one time in the New Testament when the disciples ask Jesus to teach them something. They had obviously watched his life, they had seen the miracles, they had noticed the authority and the wonderful way he spoke. Again and again, they must have asked themselves what the secret of this life was. The thing that obviously struck them was that he kept disappearing every so often to spend time with his Father. He seemed to have this permanent and natural relationship with God which they must have envied and wanted themselves.

When they said: 'O Lord, teach us to pray,' Jesus gave them a surprising answer. He began by saying, 'Pray like this. Our Father who is in heaven. . . .' In other words he was saying that if you want to learn how to pray it has got to come out of a relationship, and when you understand the relationship you know how to pray. When you see that God is your Father, you have begun to grasp the whole essence of prayer. It is not a technique, method or system, but is merely a product of a relationship.

In fact it has two parts to it as it includes both being and saying. One part involves just enjoying the company of God and the other involves talking to him and listening. Both of these are natural parts of any good relationship. In fact, interestingly enough, one of the characteristics of a close relationship is that two people can be together without talking and not feel embarrassed. There is a prevailing feeling that if you are going to pray you have actually got to say something or maybe God will go off and do something else!

One of the things that flows naturally out of my relationship with my own children is that we want to spend time together and talk about all sorts of things. We have never read books about it. We have never been instructed by anybody else on it. We just seem to do it naturally. In fact, the more time we spend together the closer we become and the greater understanding we have of each other.

It would be strange if one day I said to my children: 'Because we have such a special relationship I believe that our times together must reflect how special it is. In order to make them really meaningful we shall only talk together once a week. We will meet in the garden shed on Wednesday afternoons between the hours of four and six! Now because this relationship is extra special, we won't talk in ordinary English but in Latin!'

Of course that is a ludicrous suggestion. We talk together when we want to and when we have something to say about any subject that is on our minds. It is in fact the most natural thing to do. I do try to spend time with the children just talking to them individually but, as well as these special occasions, if there is any time during the day when they want to ask me something they are free to do so.

Can you imagine one of my children coming up to me while we are out shopping one day and saying: 'Gracious father, I wish to bring before thee a humble petition and ask that thou wilt grant my request. I would be grateful if we could purchase some edible tubers, fragmented and subsequently immersed in a seething emollient fluid, transmogrified into brittle morsels of an amber hue!' It is much more likely that he would say: 'Dad, can I have some chips!'

When a friend of mine went for a job interview not long ago he went to the man's home because this was the most convenient place to meet. He entered the study of this eminent gentleman who was seated behind a large desk. My friend sat nervously on the edge of a chair in front of the desk trying his best to answer questions respectfully and correctly. Suddenly, in the middle of the conversation, the door of the study burst open and a scruffy five-year-old boy ran in across the carpet and leapt straight into the arms of this man. The small boy, who was obviously his son, gave his dad an enormous hug and said: 'Dad, when are we going fishing?' The father encouraged the boy, in no uncertain terms, to go out of the study until he had finished the interview. It was quite obvious, however, that this little boy had a relationship with that man which was somewhat different from my friend who had come for the interview!

When Jesus taught the disciples to pray he told them to use the word 'Abba' or 'Dad'. Can it really be that Jesus encouraged us to use this most intimate term to talk to God? Yes! God, the great Creator of the universe, because of Jesus' death on the cross, has made it possible for us to be on intimate terms with him. We don't need to sit there nervously twitching on the edge of a chair wondering whether God is pleased with us, because he calls us to come running into his arms, to enjoy his presence, to open up our hearts to him and to share with him the things that are meaningful to us. This is a privilege for his children. There are many of course outside the family, in religious circles, who think they are praying but are living on presumption. It is only when you have been adopted into his family, committing your life to him, that you are free to have access to him.

He is not the slightest bit impressed with so much of the waffle in our prayers—most of which we include in an attempt to somehow make God feel that we are good Christians. Paul uses the same term 'Abba' in Romans when he says:

> When we cry, 'Abba! Father!' it is the Spirit himself bearing witness with our spirit that we are children of God, and if children, then heirs, heirs of God and fellow heirs with

Christ, provided we suffer with him in order that we may also be glorified with him (Romans 8:15–17).

Of course, we are not to be flippant or stupid but respectful in the presence of God. We are his children and he has things he wants to say to us and wants us to be real and open with him. We don't have to go to a special building to pray and we don't have to speak in a special language. We don't even have to talk in a particular manner. All we have to do is to be ourselves whenever we can and wherever we are.

I remember visiting a prison once and talking to a prisoner about prayer. He had become a Christian a few days before. When I suggested we prayed, he didn't even close his eyes! (It's funny how we assume there is a right and wrong position to adopt when talking to God.) He then talked to God as if he were talking to me. He spoke in the most free and easy way, swearing like a trooper as he went! As he had not been a Christian very long, swear words were still part of his vocabulary. If he had cut them out he would have been very short of things to say! Now, had he gone on swearing years later that wouldn't have been a good thing, but I believe that God was thrilled with his prayer. He wasn't offended by the words he used (after all it wasn't the first time God had heard them!), but he listened to his heart and his heart was being expressed to God in a way that was honest and open.

When Jesus talked about prayer in Matthew 6 he was obviously tired of all the claptrap of the Pharisees who used eloquent phrases and made such a show of their praying so that everybody would be impressed with them. You can detect in his teaching a longing for ordinary people just to be open and natural with their heavenly Father. They don't have to feel that every time they come to God he is weighing what they say (other Christians might be but he certainly isn't). They don't have to make sure that they say it properly so that he is pleased. He just wants to enjoy their company and wants them to open up their hearts to him. It is honesty that God wants because he knows our hearts before we start anyway. So there is not much point in trying to cover up, pretending we are feeling something that we are not.

Prayer meetings can be so forced and formal. I can think of many times when I have been in a prayer meeting and spent half the time trying to work out a prayer that I felt would be acceptable to everyone around me. Only then could I safely pray. I would be just about to open my mouth to pray and somebody else would jump in and pray the same prayer! It is all rather hard work—especially when so many prayers are either indirect preaching, or putting the last prayer right! Let's just talk to Jesus.

Jesus did in fact put aside times when he went to be alone with his Father. We would do well to find time in our own busy schedule just to sit in his presence for a while. So often I personally come to God because of what I want or because I want to hear instructions from him. But I do believe his greatest longing is that I just come and be with him. God does want to speak to us, but very often the things he wants to speak to us about are not matters of guidance but about himself. God wants us to read his word and to spend time with him, just so he can share with us what he is like.

This is not intended to be a comprehensive statement about prayer. It is just to say that when we understand and grasp, not only with our minds but with our hearts, that the Creator of the universe is our Father then the natural result is that we can be free to talk to him about anything. We have to cultivate the practice of talking to him and sharing with him right through the day, whenever the opportunity is there.

It must be true too that God doesn't just want us to ask for things, but he does actually want to enjoy our company and for us to enjoy his. Many marriage relationships go wrong because the only communication is discussion about the family—the things they are going to do and where they are going to go. Relationships really become meaningful when two people can open up and talk about themselves and the things that are real to them. They get to a point where they really want to enjoy each other's company and just be together.

I am sure it is true that God wants us to feel free to ask him about anything at any time, and most of us really fail to do that. We get ourselves in a terrible mess over so many things and it never occurs to us that maybe we could simply ask God about it. We seem to take every other means to find the answer to the things that crop up during the day instead of very simply stopping and asking the Father for his help. It certainly would make life a great deal simpler for many of us if we began to do that.

But surely God wants more than that. He must really long for us to open up to him so that he can share his heart with us. He wants to be able to share with us how he feels about his world and his church, as well as about us and the people with whom we have contact. Prayer is not just a one way conversation. It is God talking to us and us talking to him. And if we want to know what God is feeling about anything we will need to spend time with him and show him that we actually want to know him and enjoy him for his own sake. Many of the questions we have to ask God about guidance would probably never need to be asked if we were building our relationship closer with him. Those sort of things would tend to be a natural consequence of our relationship.

Nobody likes to have friendships where they know that a person is only their friend for what they can get out of them. We appreciate real friendships when we know the other person actually wants our company. I am sure that is why the psalmist said he wanted to seek God's face. He didn't just want to go to God to get what he could from him, but he wanted to see him, to know him and just enjoy him. This isn't something that comes easy to most of us, but it may be that we need to discipline ourselves in order to cultivate that sort of relationship. And surely we will know that if we really are enjoying God's presence day by day then when he does have something to say to us he will be able to say it. He won't have to wait until the next time that we have set aside specifically for prayer, but he will know that he can get through to us whenever he wants to.

God on the lookout!

In the last chapter of his book *Fear No Evil*, David Watson shared an encounter with God that we would all do well to take very seriously indeed.

> Between one and three a.m. God spoke to me so powerfully and painfully that I have never felt so broken before him (and still do).
>
> He showed me that all my preaching, writing and other ministry was absolutely nothing compared to my love relationship with him. In fact my sheer busyness had squeezed out the close intimacy I had known with him during the first few months of the year after my operation. [*Fear No Evil*, Hodder & Stoughton 1984.]

There are a lot of us who could identify with that if we were to be honest enough to do so. We are so caught up and involved with our busyness for God that our relationship with him slips back. God is much more concerned to find worshippers than workers. If we really know how to worship then our work will flow from that.

From time to time in the gospels Jesus gives us a glimpse of what God is feeling. Isn't it always a very special thing when a person shares with you something from deep within their heart? I suppose that is because it means they have been able to exercise a certain amount of trust in you. When you get a glimpse in the New Testament of the feelings of God it is something that is very special and also something that we should take very seriously.

When Jesus is talking to the woman at the well, he says: 'But the hour is coming, and now is, when the true worshippers will worship the Father in spirit and truth, for such the Father seeks to worship him. God is spirit, and those who worship him must worship in spirit and truth' (John 4:23–24). Jesus tells us that God the Father is on the lookout for worshippers, real worshippers. In the Bible we are told that we should praise the Lord. Praise is something that all of us are commanded to do. The very creation is commanded to praise God. God commands praise but he seeks worship.

Worship is not something we can do unless it is done out of freedom to choose. We have often confused worship with singing choruses, playing music and all the other things that are associated with meetings. But in reality these are only an expression of worship. Worship itself is far deeper than that and has to do with the heart. In fact the first mention of worship in the Bible comes in Genesis 22:5. Abraham says to his servant: 'Stay here with the ass; I and the lad will go yonder and worship, and come again to you.' Abraham didn't take with him the conventional instruments of worship. (Today it would be a tambourine, guitar and songbook—plus supplement!) He took a knife and wood for a fire—as well as his only son! Now these are the instruments of death and sacrifice. In other words, real worship has to do with laying down everything that we have and putting to death our lives in the service of God. Isn't that why Paul said: 'I appeal to you therefore, brethren, by the mercies of God, to present your bodies as a living sacrifice, holy and acceptable to God, which is your spiritual worship' (Romans 12:1)?

To an eastern person, the position of the body in worship reflects the attitude of the heart. He would lie prostrate before God as an act of submission and of giving himself. What we do with our bodies physically reflects a great deal of what is going on in our hearts. Worship has to do with the prostration of our lives before God. Any worship that is going to be real has got to start with the commitment of our lives.

Jesus went on to say that the sort of worship God is looking for is that of the spirit. When our spirit is united with his spirit we can express that sense of adoration, love and self-giving. When the heart is right we can express ourselves in songs, bodily movement, or in whatever way is most meaningful. In other words we will sing choruses or songs, raise our hands, or whatever, but these things are merely an expression of what is going on in our hearts.

Many of us are beginning to learn to be free in our expression as well as in our emotions. Emotionalism, which means the emotions are taking the lead, of course is not a good thing. It is a state of unhealthy imbalance. But God has given us our emotions and he wants them to be free.

How can you fall in love with someone without involving the emotions? There is something very horrible about worship that has no emotion in it at all. Maybe some of us need to be a little less embarrassed and contained in our expressions of love towards God.

If I told you that although I was in love with my wife I was much too embarrassed to put my arms around her, kiss her, or hold her tight, you would think there was something very strange about me. Certainly you would think I needed prayer! I often wonder how God feels when he looks down upon us in our static formalism, expressing words that our hearts and bodies seem to be totally unable to communicate. We have all been put off by wild extremes, but that is often an excuse. Isn't it strange that the majority of us would be more than happy to go to a barn dance and really enjoy ourselves, and yet in the context of worship we find it almost offensive. Jesus had to rebuke the Pharisees in Matthew 15:7–8, 'You hypocrites! Well did Isaiah prophesy of you, when he said: "This people honours me with their lips, but their heart is far from me."' It is reminiscent of Jeremiah who said to God of the children of Israel: 'Thou art near in their mouth and far from their hearts.' When God is near in our hearts then he will be near in our mouths.

Jesus also said that worship needs to be true. It means that what we say is what we feel and what we know in our experience. An act of praise is somewhat different because it is making a statement about God which is true however we feel about him. He is King whether we feel it or not. But worship moves into a heart expression of love and therefore needs to be true—otherwise it is hypocrisy. There is a world of difference between a fellow who turns to his girlfriend and says: 'I love you,' but deep inside he is really saying: 'I want you, and I know that by saying these words it will help me to get what I want,' and the one who says: 'I love you,' and his whole life is an expression of the reality of that love in self-giving. Jesus in fact said that the test of love is not what you say but what you do. He said: 'If you love me you will keep my commandments (John 14:15). It really is as simple as that.

Jesus was continually contrasting the worship of the Pharisees, which was an outward show and consisted of a multitude of words which had no depth at all, with the true worship that God desired. What he is saying is that God the Father is not looking for Sunday worshippers or church attenders. He is not interested in people's nice clean clothes and smart appearance, or their religious expression, but he is looking for people whose hearts are towards him in whatever place and situation they find themselves. That, he says, is true worship. It has nothing to do with buildings or holy places or even meetings. It has to do with an openness of heart and a love for God the Father. The Father must be so tired of the emptiness of what we say and do in the name of worship.

People talk quite a bit today about the church being the bride. The emphasis is usually put on the fact that a bride is beautiful and prepared for the bridegroom—just as God is preparing his church. Although that is true, really the greatest characteristic of a bride is that she is in love. I know that may sound obvious, but if so, isn't that surely what God is looking for in his church? We might have a church that is beautifully organized and is structurally perfect but fails to be what God is looking for. He is actually looking for a people who are in love with him. When Jesus speaks to the Ephesian church in the book of Revelation he commends it for a great deal of the good things seen there, but his great desire for them is that they regain the love they had had at first. Can you and I honestly say that we are in love with Jesus?

Sometimes when I have been away and come home, the most wonderful thing for me, apart from seeing my wife again, is to see the expressions on my children's faces when they see me for the first time. There is such a genuine joy at being reunited. It really is a marvellous thing.

Usually when I have been away I bring something back and there is always excitement in that too. I hope though that the day will never come when the first thing they do when they see me is to ask what I have brought. They might even get to the point of being glad that I go because I bring things home!

A father loves to receive love from his children and to know that he is loved for who he is and not for what he can provide. We don't really have to worry about God providing for our needs. We do need to concentrate though on our heart attitude towards God and ask that by his Spirit we might be lovers again, falling deeply in love with him. Then maybe our worship will begin to be in spirit and in truth, and the Father will have found what he is looking for.

8

A Father Who Disciplines

Some years ago we lived in a house with a small garden containing one tree. It was supposed to be an apple tree, but it very rarely produced any fruit. On more than one occasion we were tempted to cut it down as it proved increasingly difficult to play football around it! I lost count of the number of times I skinned my head on the branches trying to chase after a ball. But it was the only tree we had and we thought that at least one tree was better than no trees at all.

On one occasion a friend came to stay with us for a few days. When it was time for her to leave, her parents came to pick her up. We invited them in for coffee and since it was such a beautiful day we went out into the garden. I disappeared into the house to put the kettle on and I suppose I must have been gone about fifteen minutes. When I returned to the garden with the tray of coffee and biscuits, I nearly dropped it out of sheer amazement at the sight which confronted me. What had happened to my apple tree? (And remember it was our only tree. When you only have one tree you can become very fond of it!) One side of the tree had been completely shorn. It was like a man with a beard that had been shaved on one side only. All around the bottom of the tree were cut branches and leaves. The father of this friend of ours was standing by the tree with a pair of secateurs in his hand, looking very pleased with himself.

I have to admit to being absolutely furious. This man, whom I had never seen before, had come to my house, and while I was getting his coffee and biscuits had destroyed half of my only tree! My only consolation was that I had got there in time to stop him damaging the rest of it!

'Do you know what kind of tree this is?' he asked me, as if I were some sort of idiot. I thought it might have been a bit more appropriate if he had asked me what sort of tree it had been rather than what sort of tree it was, but nevertheless I replied that as far as I knew it was an apple tree.

'Has it ever produced any apples?' he asked me. I didn't much like the manner in which he questioned me, but I had to admit to him that we had only had a few apples from the tree. (I should have said one or two which might have been a bit more accurate.) He then went on to comment that the tree would never produce any fruit in its present state because it needed drastic pruning. He then continued with tremendous confidence to tell me that I was now responsible for cutting the other half of the tree.

When he had gone I took Lois on one side and had a quiet word with her about this extraordinary visitor. Actually he was very nice and a delightful person, but I had been rather taken aback by this opening encounter with him. She reassured me that in fact by profession he was an expert on fruit trees. And as you have no doubt guessed, the following year we had far more apples on that tree than I had ever seen before. I had learned a lesson on that occasion, namely that pruning is a vital part of bearing fruit.

Somebody once said that you need to get your worst

enemy to prune your roses. I remember going out to prune ours once, and when I had finished Lois asked why I had not yet pruned the roses! She went out to do it and, being far more ruthless in these things than I am, cut them down till they were almost non-existent. However, it seemed to do the trick and we produced very good roses that year. Drastic action has to be taken if we want to produce really good fruit and flowers. So it is in the Christian life. God has to apply the knife in areas of our life to make us the sort of people he wants us to be.

There is a wonderful phrase in John 15 when Jesus talks to the disciples and gives them a picture of what the church of Jesus Christ is like. He describes it as a vine and how we are the branches of the vine. Right at the beginning of that picture he says that his Father is the vinedresser (or gardener). This means that God has responsibility as a father to enable us to produce fruit in our lives. If we ask him to do it we must be careful not to argue with his methods. He is the expert.

Now it is impossible to experience the fruit of the Spirit in a vacuum. You can't really know the joy of the Lord unless you know something of suffering. You can't understand patience unless you are in a situation which requires you to be patient. You can't know the supernatural love of God flowing through you unless you meet those who are unlovable. As God wants to produce the character of Jesus in each of us, so he has to take us through difficult and hard times in order for us to learn what it is to trust him and to look to him for power in our lives. We must get beyond our natural human resources in order to begin to rely on his divine resources.

God works in our lives in these ways both to enable us to be fruitful and also to bring about the discipline we need. Suffering is going to be a part of the Christian experience, partly because we live in a sinful world and partly because it enables us to become more like Jesus. God will take the circumstances of our lives and use them for the creative purpose of changing us into his likeness. Sometimes this will mean the taking away of things that are harmful. What is harmful for one person may not be for another, but God alone knows what needs to be removed from our lives. Sometimes these things appear to us to be essential and good. When we believe that, it is much more difficult to receive and accept the discipline of God. Think about these verses from Romans 5:3–5, 'More than that, we rejoice in our sufferings, knowing that suffering produces endurance ... and endurance does not disappoint us, because God's love has been poured into our hearts through the Holy Spirit which has been given to us.' Or again note the words of Jesus in Luke 21:16–19, 'You will be delivered up even by parents and brothers and kinsmen and friends, and some of you they will put to death; you will be hated by all for my name's sake. But not a hair of your head will perish. By your endurance you will gain your lives.'

Suffering and difficulties in our lives, when seen under the loving fatherly hand of God, will always be working positively in our favour even though we may not understand it at the time. Peter wrote: 'In this you rejoice, though now for a little while you may have to suffer various trials, so that the genuineness of your faith, more precious than gold which though perishable is tested by fire, may redound to praise and glory and honour at the revelation of Jesus Christ' (1 Peter 1:6–7). Here again we come up with the same relationship between fatherhood and the kingdom. If we are going to live in the kingdom we have to live in obedience to the King, and often he will arrange things in our lives, or ask us to do things which we don't actually agree with. From his perspective though these things will be working positively for the kingdom of God.

Now here is a challenging question. Do we believe this Bible statement, 'We know that in everything God works for good with those who love him, who are called according to his purpose' (Romans 8:28)? If we as Christians believe that God's word is true and that therefore this statement is true, there are certain consequences involved. It means that we can never complain or grumble again, because complaining and grumbling are totally inconsistent with this truth.

For many of us complaining is a way of life. I once asked a friend how he was feeling and he said, 'I can't complain...unfortunately!' But if all things, not just some things, *all* things are being used by God for our good then we can't complain about anything that happens to us! (Note that this scripture is written in the context of prayer. It is assuming that our lives are lived in that sense of prayer expressed in a daily calling out to God, and a confidence that Jesus intercedes for us.) It means that the only choice for us in the good times and in the bad is to do what Paul recommends in 1 Thessalonians 5:16–18, 'Rejoice always, pray constantly, give thanks in all circumstances; for this is the will of God in Christ Jesus for you.' It is, of course, much easier to believe this when everything is going well. It is when times are hard that we often wonder whether God cares about us at all. It is because we are God's children that these things are allowed to happen in our lives.

It would be good to read this familiar passage carefully and think about it.

> And have you forgotten the exhortation which addresses you as sons? 'My son, do not regard lightly the discipline of the Lord, nor lose courage when you are punished by him.

> For the Lord disciplines him whom he loves, and chastises every son whom he receives.' It is for discipline that you have to endure. God is treating you as sons; for what son is there whom his father does not discipline? If you are left without discipline, in which all have participated, then you are illegitimate children and not sons. Besides this, we have had earthly fathers to discipline us and we respected them. Shall we not much more be subject to the Father of spirits and live? For they disciplined us for a short time at their pleasure, but he disciplines us for our good, that we may share his holiness. For the moment all discipline seems painful rather than pleasant; later it yields the peaceful fruit of righteousness to those who have been trained by it (Hebrews 12:5–11).

There are many things which happen in our home regarding discipline that our children find very difficult to accept are really working for their good. But as their father I have a responsibility to help mould the characters of my children—to bring them up as mature adults with good and positive moral qualities. In order to bring this about in a person's life there has to be discipline. So it is in the family of God. Many of the people who have most clearly expressed the life of Christ in our own generation have been those who have suffered a great deal. We have all been captivated by the life and experience of somebody like Corrie ten Boom who has been such a witness to the reality of Christ. Yet it was through the suffering she experienced that she found this depth of relationship and God was able to mould her character to become more like his.

When the children of Israel came out of Egypt they experienced a most tremendous miracle at the Red Sea. As the waters were parted and they went through on dry land they turned and saw the destruction of the Egyptians. No wonder they celebrated with such exuberance and excitement. There on the shores of the sea they enjoyed a most wonderful act of worship and praise. They were so thrilled with the goodness of God and all he had done for them. As they had stood there on the shore with the Egyptian army behind and the sea ahead of them, disaster had suddenly turned into an amazing victory. One moment they thought they would be utterly destroyed and the next they were seeing the total annihilation of their enemy and knew they were free from oppressive slavery for ever.

In Exodus 15 we read of the song that the people sang. Then verse 22 says: 'Then Moses led Israel onward from the Red Sea, and they went into the wilderness of Shur; they went three days in the wilderness and found no water.' It seemed such a hard and difficult thing for them to understand that the same God who had enabled them to walk through the water, acting with miraculous power to destroy their enemy, was allowing them to go through a period of terrible hardship.

In fact their whole experience in the wilderness was one of testing. We read that again and again during that period they began to grumble and complain. They were failing to learn the lessons God was wanting to teach them. That time in the wilderness was to be a time when they relearned their dependence on God.

For generations they had been slaves in Egypt, and during that time they had forgotten what it was to be utterly dependent upon the living God. All that their forefathers, Abraham, Isaac, and Jacob had learned had been lost in Egypt. Even if it was remembered as history, it was lost in terms of experience. If they were to enter into the promised land and enjoy its fruits and to survive as a nation, they had to re-establish that utter, daily dependence on God as their Father. God had intended that they would learn these lessons in a very short period, but in the end it took them forty years. Further on in that particular story we read how God produced a miraculous answer to their need. Doesn't that remind us of ourselves? The same pattern seems to be repeated in us. But it doesn't have to be the case if we understand what God is doing.

Learning to fly

In Deuteronomy 32, when Moses is reminding the children of Israel of all that happened to them, he gives this beautiful picture in verse 11: 'Like an eagle that stirs up its nest, that flutters over its young, spreading out its wings, catching them, bearing them on its pinions, the Lord alone did lead him, and there was no foreign god with him.'

God was teaching the children of Israel to fly and to be dependent on him. In the same way as an eagle rides the thermals so we are to learn to ride in the Spirit of God. An eagle doesn't flap or wave its wings around. It glides by moving in currents of air. God wants us to learn what it is to live in the Spirit, trusting in him day by day. The Lord pushes us out of our cosy positions to teach us to fly. Testing times are learning experiences to enable us to be people of faith.

All of us have lived part of our lives without God. We have built up patterns in our lives which mean that our security is in the things of this world. It is with this in mind that, day by day, God takes us through the hard times, and disciplines us in order that we might relearn and rediscover that our security and source of supply is the living God. This must cease to be a theory and become a reality. God wants a people whose total dependence is on him. If we want to be part of it we have to go through the training course.

The potter

Another interesting picture the Bible uses to describe our relationship with God, and his work in our lives, is that of a potter and his clay. The potter with firm and yet gentle movements of his hands moulds the supple clay into the shapes he wants to make. The hands that mould us and change us are the strong, firm, gentle hands of a father. They are not the hands of violence or aggression, seeking to do harm, but they are hands that desire to mould and to produce something beautiful. The responsibility of the clay is to allow the potter to do whatever he wants to do. Our responsibility is to stop fighting and resisting God, and allow him to work out his purposes in our lives. Isn't this a marvellous picture:

> Woe to him who strives with his Maker, an earthen vessel with the potter! Does the clay say to him who fashions it, 'What are you making'? or 'Your work has no handles'?
>
> Woe to him who says to a father, 'What are you begetting?' or to a woman, 'With what are you in travail?'
>
> Thus says the Lord, the Holy One of Israel, and his Maker: 'Will you question me about my children, or command me concerning the work of my hands? I made the earth, and created man upon it; it was my hands that stretched out the heavens, and I commanded all their host.' [Isaiah 45:9–12.]

It is very easy to find ourselves complaining to God not only about what he is doing with our lives but about the gifts with which he has or has not endowed us. Problems of inadequacy bother most of us from time to time. We easily become swamped with a sense of our own inability and weakness. The truth is that God has given us everything we have and therefore we have everything we need to fulfil the work to which he has called us. He has made us in a particular way with particular gifts which will enable us to fulfil our calling. Our only responsibility is to use fully what we have been given in the service of God. When we stand before God we will not be asked to give account for the things that other people were able to do, but we will be held responsible for the use of what God has given us.

Instead of complaining about what we have or don't have it might be better just to rejoice in it and to get on and use our gifts fully for him. Notice James 1:2–4, 'Consider it pure joy, my brothers, whenever you face trials of many kinds, because you know that the testing of your faith develops perseverance. Perseverance must finish its work so that you may be mature and complete, not lacking anything' (NIV). How do you and I react to trials? Usually, I suspect, with a survival mentality that reckons we need to grin and bear it and we'll just make it through. James says: 'Consider it pure joy!'

If we want to be mature and our faith to be strong, it has to be tested. These times of testing are not easy, but if we see them in this light it certainly makes it easier.

Life in the Spirit

How you behave and act in the Christian life depends very much on your view of God's involvement with the world. As already mentioned there are really two main alternatives. The first is that God exists and although we can have a living relationship with him, he is not directly involved in his world. We can be absolutely sure of heaven when we know that we have received Christ's forgiveness, but meanwhile it is up to us to make the most of what we have here on earth. He expects us to go and work for him here in this world—which means that we have to do as much as possible to extend the kingdom of God. The initiative in this instance remains primarily with us and we have to do as much as we can to further God's work. A large amount of Christian activity at a personal and corporate level stems from this view.

The second alternative is that God *is* deeply involved in his world, that he is always wanting to initiate, he is working according to his own plans and his desire for us is merely that we co-operate with what he is already doing.

As you read through the Bible you find the account of a God who is deeply involved in his world and is continually taking initiatives. In fact, God is working according to a great master plan. We read in Ephesians 1:10 of a 'plan for the fullness of time, to unite all things in him, things in heaven and things on earth'. We can, of course, either choose to be part of God's purposes or to rebel against them. That is reflected in how we respond to the message of the kingdom. Ever since the fall, God has been working in the world to bring about the whole process of restoration and reconciliation. Throughout the Old Testament there were great waves of initiative taken by God in this restoration process.

First of all he appointed a man, Abraham, in whom he could express his will and purpose, and through whom he could bless his world. Out of that one man he formed a nation. Through this nation he wanted to express what he was like and to be a blessing to the whole world. It was to be a nation in whom he could demonstrate the principles of the kingdom of God lived out on earth. As we go through the Old Testament we see these waves of restoration. There is the movement of the children of Israel out of Egypt and then their going into exile and being restored. There is the initiative taken with the prophets. Then the great climax with the birth of Jesus and the coming of the kingdom in power and reality.

There follows the Acts of the Apostles and the outpouring of the Holy Spirit and the beginning of the church. Then the great missionary endeavours through Paul and the other apostles. Finally moving into church history there have been great movements restoring God's purposes in the earth.

Each of these movements of the Spirit of God have required men's co-operation and commitment, but God has been the prime mover. For example, it was not the idea of the children of Israel to leave Egypt and cross the Red Sea, nor was it their decision to go and live in the land of Canaan. In fact, nowhere is there any indication that they sat down to mark out a plan of action to get them out of Egypt and into the promised land. God had already worked out exactly how it was to be done. All he needed was to find a man or men who would be willing to listen to him, to get caught up in his vision and to follow his plans.

At times throughout the Old Testament we have many glimpses of individuals who were men of God's heart, that is, they were primarily wanting to find out what God was doing and then join in. They were not restricted by their own human limitations or their own experience. They believed in a God with whom nothing was impossible and began to open their minds and hearts to all the possibilities. They began to walk and to live in faith as they heard God's word speaking to them. That is why you find David continually turning to God before a battle to find out whether or not there was going to be victory that day. He would only go out if he knew God's hand was upon him. The greatest trouble occurred in the promised land when we read that 'each man did what was right in his own eyes'.

We all of us need to know that God has a purpose and a plan for each of our lives today. The living God is on the move today right across the world—both on a global scale and at an individual and local level. God is bringing in his kingdom. He is working according to his own purposes and plans. He is a God who is initiating and moving forward. That is why the church can never be a static thing because God is always on the move. It is tremendously exciting to grasp with our hearts and minds that the God whom we worship, believe and trust is a God who is active in our world. It then means that the main question we need to ask is: 'What is God doing?' and join him. There of course is a danger in this, namely to assume that all we have to do is sit and do nothing, or perhaps to spend all day waiting for a whisper to come into our minds before we act. No, God is wanting us to have a heart desiring to move forward and to be involved with him in his world. God's word seems to come to those who are willing to be obedient and to act, but we do have a responsibility to listen before we rush around assuming what God wants us to do. Remember these amazing words of Jesus:

> Truly, truly, I say to you, the Son can do nothing of his own accord, but only what he sees the Father doing; for whatever he does, that the Son does likewise. For the Father loves the Son, and shows him all that he himself is doing; and greater works than these will he show him, that you may marvel (John 5:19–20).

When Joshua crossed over into the promised land we read that he met a man with a sword in his hand. The Bible records that Joshua turned to this individual and said to him: 'Are you for us or for our adversaries?' The reply came back: 'No. But as commander of the army of the Lord I have now come.' In other words he was saying the issue is not whether I am with you or against you—the real question is: 'Are you with me?' Again and again we say to God either consciously or unconsciously: 'Are you with us in this venture? Will you bless us in what we are doing?' The whole question needs to be reversed because God is saying to us today, both individually and corporately, 'Are you with me?' If Jesus' priority was to do what he saw the Father doing and to say things that he knew the Father wanted said, how much more should that be our priority.

If we examine the life of the average Christian today, or the average Christian congregation, we have to admit that there is a tremendous amount of activity. We seem able to fill all our spare moments with good religious activity. The church programme is usually full. Every night of the week there is some event or other and we find ourselves with a full diary for nearly a year ahead! Those churches can certainly not be accused of doing nothing. However, if we look at the productivity generated out of that activity, we have to admit that there is something sadly lacking.

Jesus is the head of the church. Therefore this means he himself wants to initiate and give direction to the church's life. It means that our prime responsibility is to hear what God is saying to us and to do it. This may take tremendous courage as we will have to cease a number of things we are already doing in order to do the one thing that he wants us to do. Maybe we should be honest and examine our own lives and the life of our fellowship. This is not intended to bring guilt and confusion to our hearts. However, if you and I are to be really honest, we must question how much of what we are involved in, and how much of what our church is involved in, has really been initiated from heaven. It is not necessarily an easy question to answer, but it is very much easier to do things because they have always been done. In fact in the Christian life it is very much easier to start things than to stop them. We need to hear God when he tells us to start and we equally need to hear him when he orders us to stop. I wouldn't for a moment want to pretend that hearing God is necessarily as easy as some people make out, but I do believe that if our hearts are really wanting to know what God is saying to us then we will hear. He is much keener for us to hear him than we are to listen so he will take steps to ensure that we understand what is required of us.

Some time ago I was in a prayer meeting where we were earnestly asking the Lord to provide the finances and the resources for a particular project. As I was praying I found God speaking to my heart and asking the question: 'Did I or did I not initiate this project?' I realized that if God had initiated this plan then he was bound to provide the resources and the funds. Can you imagine God telling you to do something and not equipping you to do it? We, of course, need to ask him how he intends to provide the funds and if there is anything we need to do, but if he begins something then he will fund it. If he had not initiated this particular project we would have been best to stop it immediately. Once we have come to the conclusion that God has begun something then we can aim our prayers in the right direction. We don't have to waste time just praying for resources for an event, we can begin to pray for the object of that particular event.

In other words, if we were running a mission we could begin to concentrate on praying for the lost as a prime directive of our requests. So many prayer letters and prayer lists are taken up with money, personnel and the logistics of administration. It appears that the lost are mentioned almost as an afterthought somewhere at the bottom of the list. In fact if God tells us to have a mission, the main directive of our prayers should be for those outside the kingdom of God, remembering constantly that God will always provide for that which he begins. That doesn't mean we should be irresponsible with regard to finance, and it may be that God will tell us to take some particular action, but it needs to be he who shows us what to do.

What does it mean then to be living in the Spirit? It means to realize that God has a purpose and a direction for our lives and that our desire is to flow along in the centre of his will. We go back again to our picture of eagles caught up in the thermal currents. It is said that when an eagle is approaching a storm he doesn't flap his wings and try to get away from it as fast as possible. He has a mechanism whereby he locks his wings into a fixed position and faces the storm head on. As he does so the thermals lift him up right over the top of the storm and he is protected. In the same way, if we lock ourselves into the purposes and the love of God, we will find that he takes us over the storms of life. The choice is either to soar like an eagle or flap like a pelican!

This means that we must answer the question as to whether, ultimately, we desire the will of God for our lives. Once that is settled in the affirmative we will find we don't have to look to God outside of ourselves to guide us, but we can listen confidently to the indwelling Spirit of God speaking to our hearts day by day. We will find that our lives are being led in the right direction because that is the longing of our hearts. We can be confident that the Father is directing us each day.

God's prime way of leading his children is through his indwelling Spirit. The word of God through the Bible comes and speaks to us directly, usually as an encouragement and confirmation. The prophetic gifts and the circumstances of our lives are also used by God to confirm what he is saying to us. If we look to circumstances as the prime means of guidance though, we will be continually buffeted about. We will find ourselves ever looking to see what circumstances bring or reading the Bible to try to find a verse that will speak to us about a particular issue. We need to learn to respond to the Spirit of God dwelling within us, and then we will find that God will confirm what he is saying to us in his own way.

Of course, there are dangers involved with this—the main one being that we could make sudden impetuous decisions which are not carefully thought through. God rarely asks us to act on impulse. We need to learn when the Spirit of God is speaking to us and when it is our own spirit. The best test of this is usually time. We must allow time for this concept to strengthen and grow in us. We should never be ashamed or frightened to share what we feel God is saying and we should allow the matter to come under the scrutiny of others whom we respect and trust, and for it to be confirmed by them.

Do you love me?

That is the most penetrating question of all. Jesus gave a very simple guideline to see if we really love him or not. It does not depend on emotion or feelings. It has nothing to do with circumstances, pressures or anything like that. If it did our love for him would be a changing, fluctuating thing. He said very simply, 'If you love me keep my commandments.' In other words if we love him we'll do what he says. That is so simple and straightforward but so very challenging.

Many times I have said to my kids: 'Have you done what I asked you?' and they reply with a whole list of things they have done instead. I have to repeat: 'But have you done what I asked you to do?' Christian work and activity are not necessarily what God is asking us to engage in. If we haven't sorted out other areas, they may be a cover for disobedience. For instance, 'Husbands, love your wives,' is a major priority but is often pushed into second place behind the call of ministry.

Again notice in 1 John 4:20–21, 'If anyone says, "I love God," and hates his brother, he is a liar; for he who does not love his brother whom he has seen, cannot love God whom he has not seen. And this commandment we have from him, that he who loves God should love his brother also.' Do we love God according to that definition?

Very simply, God longs to receive from us a response of love. That love is expressed in the little daily things of life by doing what he wants us to do, reacting how he wants us to react and being what he wants us to be. The Christian, as a child of God, demonstrates the degree of his love for God by his willingness to obey.

9

Father and His Family

As God is Father then it means the church by definition is a family. In most human families, the greatest problems occur between the brothers and sisters in that family. They didn't choose each other. Their common factor is their parents and they are put together and have to work out relationships wholly through much pain and laughter. The family bond keeps them together but, as all parents know, it isn't always easy. So it is in the family of God.

Jesus rarely talked about the church. He mainly spoke of the kingdom of God. The church is the corporate human expression of the kingdom. It consists of men and women who are part of the kingdom of God living in relationship with one another, because those who have become members of the kingdom are automatically a part of the family. If you are a subject of the King you are a child of the Father! So the family of God consists of all those who have been born again by the Spirit of God and have become children of the one Father.

Usually, of course, when we talk about the church it tends to be from a human perspective like a child viewing his family from his point of view—which will include all his sense of envy or strife with the other children as well as a deep awareness of belonging to each other. It is interesting to try and look at the church from a divine viewpoint, that is, to see how God sees it. God must look at his family and see a great deal that makes him happy and a lot that makes him sad. He must long for us really to be a family in the fullest possible sense.

From his perspective it means that the family of God is all embracing as it includes every Christian. (To discover how to enter into such a relationship you need to look at the last chapter!) Most of us can only see the church from our own viewpoint. That is, we look at it from where we are and through the group of people with whom we have fellowship. But if we want to see the church as God sees it, then we will need to see the whole church and long to embrace all those who belong to Christ. It doesn't mean to say that everybody is in the right place with God, nor does it mean that everybody's beliefs and doctrinal positions are correct; it does mean that all those who have the Spirit of Christ are his and therefore a part of his family.

Our responsibility, therefore, if we really want to please the Father, is to draw the family of God together and not put up new divisions between the members.

First church—Jesus' pattern

We can learn a great deal from Jesus and the relationships he had. We notice firstly, that he had a very close relationship with three people—Peter, James and John. In many ways this was an exclusive relationship. It was a deep friendship that he had with these three men and almost certainly he shared openly with them, much more closely than he did with the twelve. It really isn't possible for us to have close, open fellowship with the whole family of God. But we can do it with a small group. Often we feel guilty if we have close friends in the church, somehow assuming that it is a wrong thing to do, but Jesus had close friends. All of us need to have one or two people that we can share intimately with. These are God-given relationships in which we can be very open and honest.

Secondly, Jesus had a group of twelve that he really gave his life to and with whom he spent most of his time. If Jesus had that sort of group how much more do we need a fellowship of people of a dozen or so with whom we are in close relationship. It is interesting to notice the tremendous growth of house groups all over the world today. God is re-emphasizing again the need for this sort of fellowship. In such a desperately insecure and lonely world, institutionalism merely increases the isolation and the sense of weakness, but God is restoring his family. In the context of this family, warm caring friendship can be offered. These home groups really are the basis of the church. If only we would dare to be honest and admit that this is the real church for a lot of people. It is not the institution that is the church, it is the relationship that we build with other believers.

In those early days of the church in the first century how would you have defined the church? Was it those who met in their houses or was it the large gathering of Christians together? Surely both were expressions of the same thing. What is the church today if it is not the relationship between believers? Of course we need structure and we need authority, but these things are merely to enable us to be the church most effectively.

Thirdly, Jesus had a larger group of seventy or probably more with whom he had some relationship. Most of us not only need a small group, but we need to be part of a form of congregational life on a larger scale. If this is so, what is to be the basis of fellowship? Surely there is only one reason for fellowship and that is to be in close proximity with other members of the family. The denominational divide cannot possibly be a God-given divide. How can the family of God be divided on the basis of denominational loyalty? How can it be divided on the basis of doctrine? How can it be divided on the basis of forms of worship?

Jerusalem pattern

If we look at the Jerusalem church pattern in the early days, what was the original condition of that church? The only division was the houses in which they met! If the person was a Christian they could not possibly be excluded (except for immorality). There was no question of whether he belonged to this church or that church. He belonged to the church.

The foundation of the early church, we are told, was the apostles and the prophets. Today the foundation of the church is in practice the pastoral ministry. And because that is the foundation, and pastors very easily become rulers, there is division according to which pastor you belong to. Of course, this is not always the case but it certainly is the reason for much division in the church today. The feeling you get in many is very similar to the situation in Israel when they said, 'We want a king to rule over us.' Jesus is to be King of the church. Pastors are there to serve and to care for the sheep and to lead them to good places to feed. We need to rediscover again the prophetic and apostolic ministry in the church. Why are so many so-called apostles today actually acting in such a sectarian way instead of giving the church to Jesus?

It would seem that there are certain characteristics of genuine apostolic ministry. One is a burden for the whole church of Jesus Christ. Secondly, there will be signs confirming the call. Thirdly, he will be as concerned with pioneering and opening up new ground as he will be for working on what already exists. But the apostle or the prophet, above all, has a heart for the whole church because he shares God's heart! How can a man have a narrow attitude to the church and be a prophet!

Let me underline that I am in no way advocating that we rebel against pastors. All of us need to have clear oversight and care in our lives. In fact we need to greatly increase the pastoral ministry because we have too few people doing too big a job.

When you build the church on the basis of relationships then you have something that can never be broken. Of course we all need pastoral care and oversight, but the church is primarily based on relationships. If you feel the Father's heart you cannot continue to grieve him, but you must work to see the church become what it is, that is a family. We may need too to recognize that the family to which we belong is not necessarily the same as the denominational grouping.

Insecurity in our relationship with God leads us to find security in structures and positions. There is nothing inherently wrong with structure, because everybody needs a framework in which to exist and authority to submit to, but the more rigid a structure becomes then the further we may have gone from our ultimate trust in God the Father.

The church is intended to be a pilgrim people, always moving on, always discovering new things with new challenges of faith day by day and week by week. Their only security is in the fact that God is the Father and he is caring for them and they are part of a family of people who care. The Lord is always wanting to be creative in what he does and to give us new ventures and targets for our faith. His desire is to reach out into the rest of the community in which we live and to draw them into his kingdom. We need to be part of the sort of church that, when people look at it, they are aware of a divine commander who is unseen and yet real. They must never be able to explain the church purely in human terms. If we look like any other human organization, run and manipulated by human skills and the desires of men, then we will never have anything to say to our world. That is why some untidiness is not necessarily a bad thing and military precision and regimentation can be dangerous.

But if we can be seen to be the family of God expressing the unseen presence of the heavenly Father, the world will see and believe.

Longing for the lost

When Jesus told the story of the prodigal son he was talking as much about the nature of God as he was the problem of man's rebellion and his need of repentance. Most of the stories of Jesus are very simple but express profound truth. In this particular story of the boy who went away from his father, Jesus gives us a picture of God's relationship with man. Here, described in a very simple parable, is the whole story of this relationship. But in this story we see the picture of a God who is prepared to allow men and women freedom to choose and then to live with the consequences of that choice. We see a God who is daily looking out into his world and longing for men and women to come back into a relationship with him. Because he has given man this freedom to choose, he won't intervene and drag him back but nevertheless he longs for him to come.

Most of us only see the superficial problems of our world, but even they are enough to make us horrified at what we see. We see the news on television and we look at the newspapers. We listen to the neighbours and the gossip in the local community. We are all aware of tensions in our own lives. But God sees far more than that.

He looks down into every home and sees the happiness and the joy, but in the midst of that he sees the trauma and the terrible suffering of our world. He looks into the human heart and sees men and women struggling desperately to find meaning and purpose in their lives but unable to find the real answer. He watches them rushing around, trying to find the solution and yet always failing to discover reality. He looks into homes and sees marriages that are splitting apart and children separated from their parents. He looks into communities and sees the strife, the greed and the selfishness that separates human beings. He sees countries that are fighting each other and the terrible tensions between nations.

He sees the hungry, the desperate and the terrible suffering of the Third World. He can see at the same time the greed and the gluttony of the West and the terrible impoverishment of millions of human beings. The heart of God is broken for his world. It is not that he must fulfil a need of his own, but that he knows human beings will only find rest and peace when they come into the shelter of his love. He knows it is the only place that men and women can really discover who they were meant to be.

In order to communicate his love to his world he has always used people. In times past he used prophets to express himself through a nation, and Jesus who perfectly expressed the life of God because he was God. And then on the day of Pentecost God poured out his Spirit on a whole crowd of ordinary human beings so that through them he could bring his love to a needy world.

Today God still chooses to use people, his church—that is the living expression of his kingdom on earth—to be that instrument to communicate the love he has for his world. How sad he must be to see that so much of our energy is used up on ourselves. How much time we spend rushing around trying to reorganize and restructure the church to keep it going. He must see the church full of so much activity centred upon itself. The Bible tells us that God wants a people who are 'for his own possession'. In other words he wants a people who will be an instrument in his hand to express his love and care for a needy world. The greatest priority of the church is to be a living witness to the world around. God's love for his world is expressed in Luke 4:18. Because he is concerned for the poor, the prisoners, the blind and the oppressed, he anointed his Son. So today he anoints his church. Why? For us? No! But for the world!

The church expressed as a family with the love and care, the forgiveness and understanding built into relationships, is really the most effective means to touch the needy world. We need so much to rediscover the heart of God for his lost world and unite together in prayer, and action, so that through us as many people as possible may be reached.

I have been conscious in my own life that one of the great barriers to evangelism is the fear of rejection. Usually when we pass on a message or some news to somebody else, we weigh up in our own minds how that message is likely to be received. If we know it will be received with pleasure and warmth we are very likely to pass it on enthusiastically. But if we suspect that what we have to say could be rejected then we tend to keep it to ourselves. This is, in fact, not because we are frightened of what we have to say being rejected, but we are frightened that along with what we have to share we ourselves might experience rejection. When we communicate something that is very meaningful to us and it is rejected by others, we can easily feel that we ourselves have been rejected. And most of us cannot afford to be rejected by the world so we steer clear of being involved in anything that will bring about that sort of response.

If Jesus had been governed by such fear he would never have gone out into the world and begun to communicate the message of the kingdom. The only reason he could do it was that he knew he was secure in the love of the Father. He knew that the Father's arms upheld him and strengthened him. He knew that he was accepted by his Father and loved with an everlasting love. Unless we discover for ourselves a real security in the love of God we will always find it difficult to communicate the message of Jesus to others. A church that is secure in God's love is a church that will throw itself into service to the world and will be able to cope with the message being either accepted or rejected.

Although there is a real place for large evangelistic endeavours and events, the real evangelism will take place in the homes and in the streets of our nation. In each area, as we begin to express the love and the care that Jesus himself would want to show to our neighbours, friends and workmates, we will discover that others will be drawn in and experience this love for themselves. It is all too easy to be involved in lots of activities at church and to be sitting on lots of committees, yet never reach out to the man next door, the people we work with, the people we go to school with and others that are already touching us in everyday life. There are plenty of people all around us who are in their hearts experiencing what that prodigal son felt and are longing to come home. Maybe God could use us to simply share the message that this is possible and that God is waiting for them.

The heart of God is for a world full of lost people. If we want to share his heart that will be our concern as well. Concern leads to prayer and prayer to vision and action.

After the shake-up

The greatest need for each one of us is to find our security in God. We are to be men and women who first and foremost look to God for our sense of well-being and identity and regarding the direction of our lives. There is no greater security than that. The whole world can fall apart and every ounce of natural security that we have disappear, but if we have everything in God we will be unshakable. The more we all do this, the more we will find we are drawn deeply together. Is that what it means when the writer to the Hebrews tells us that God will again shake everything and only the unshakable kingdom of God will stand? As we build our lives and therefore our fellowship on him we will find something that is unshakable in the days ahead. And as things in this world become more and more insecure, and people feel more vulnerable and tossed around by the circumstances of life, the world will be looking for something that is strong. The kingdom of God (not the church as we know it) is the only thing that will be able to stand. Let's seek to put that first in our lives.

Let me add here that there is a balance to this teaching and it is that we need each other. We were not intended to be isolated individually. The 'me and Jesus is all I need' idea is not what it is all about. We must find our security in the Father and at the same time discover our dependence on each other. Not only is God a father, we are also a family.

10

Welcome to the Family

I sat in a restaurant recently with a young man who shared with me his most remarkable story. He told me that when he was very young his parents were separated and there was a great deal of unhappiness in the home all through his teenage years. Along with many of his friends and contemporaries he had turned to drugs and was living a fairly immoral life, but during this period of uncertainty and real unhappiness in his life he began to search for something else. In his desperation he cried out to God asking if somehow he could find the truth. Like so many, he didn't know if God existed, but he knew he longed for more than he had yet found.

Some days later he found himself up in his attic room where he would often go to get away from everybody. He was a keen drummer and as he sat playing his drums one of his drum sticks flew out of his hand and disappeared into a dark crevice on one side of the attic. As he went in search of it he found it had landed on top of a large golden-covered book which he could not recall noticing before. He took it out and began to look at it—intrigued to discover it was a Bible. As he thumbed through the pages of the New Testament he began to read and found himself absolutely captivated by what he found. It was quite different from the religion he had heard about. He was enthralled by the man Jesus. If only he could identify with his revolutionary attitude to life. This was the beginning of a search to find a personal experience of the Jesus he had read about. It was just the beginning of a whole series of events that within a short space of time led him to Christ and to a whole new life.

This of course is only one of millions of stories. Each one is different but expresses the same thing. I just love to ask people I meet to tell me something of their own story. It is amazing to hear how they found Christ. Every person comes from a different background, with different experiences, and each comes to Christ through different circumstances. Ordinary men and women, young and old, in all sorts of situations in life, are finding purpose, meaning and identity as they discover a relationship with God through Jesus.

Many people say that they are searching for God, but the staggering and almost unbelievable message of the New Testament is that it is God who is searching for us. The message Jesus brought to this world is that the God who created the universe, the all-powerful, all-knowing God is looking for men and women. He longs for the people he made to really enjoy the world that he put them in, as well as the one yet to come, and also to discover the security that they were intended to enjoy in a relationship with him. Often people say they have found God. In reality he found us. He waits for us to respond, but he has taken the initiative.

When Jesus was criticized for spending time with the sinners and the drunkards of his day, he explained his behaviour by telling a series of stories which are recorded in Luke 15. In each of these he explains that men and women are lost but God is looking for them. He goes on to reveal that in fact God will never force anyone into a relationship with himself because he has given us all free will. But he is looking and he is waiting, and will go on waiting until we are ready to respond to him.

We will never really find God until we recognize that we have a need of him. There are many barriers to our coming to that point. For some it is a strong, often unconscious, prejudice.

Prejudice is often based upon past experiences. These may be bad experiences of religion as a child or young person. It may be caused by people or places that we have associated with Christianity and these create in us a negative reaction. Most of us have prejudices of one sort or another, and the danger comes when we fail to admit it and refuse to recognize how deeply they are ingrained in us. But when we do see there just may be prejudice at work in us, we can begin to make progress.

Secondly, and probably the strongest element in each of us, is *pride.* We find it so difficult to admit that we have been wrong and have failed. This is particularly true of men and certainly it must be one of the main reasons why more women seem to become Christians than men. We hate to admit that we need someone or something else. We know perfectly well that our lives are inadequate, but somehow we would rather try and make it on our own and pull through unassisted. The truth is that we were never intended to live that way and so we never will. There are other things as well as prejudice and pride, of course, at work in us.

Fear is one of those. Many of us are afraid of what it will mean to become a Christian. We have to associate with other Christians and be known to be a follower of Jesus. Jesus always asked people to count the cost before they came and followed him. It always costs us something to be a follower of Jesus Christ. If the world hated and rejected him then that is how we may be treated, and unless we understand that to be a Christian is to be fully associated with Jesus and his lifestyle then we will be surprised when certain things happen in our lives, and the result may be that we cannot continue. It is better, Jesus said, to count the cost before you enter into this way of life.

To become a Christian is to enter the kingdom of God, that is to allow Jesus to be King in our lives. Part of the cost of being a Christian is bringing our lives under the will and purpose of God. When Jesus spoke to the rich young ruler and told him to sell everything before following him (Mark 10:17), he seemed on the surface to have had a hard attitude towards him. But he was only encouraging him to understand the real issues of what it meant to follow him. If that young man had put money first in his life (which was his particular god—it may be different for others), then he would never really be able to live in the kingdom of God. So Jesus encouraged him to get rid of the thing that ruled him so that Jesus himself could rule his life. It has always cost people to become Christians. And so it does today.

The benefits of discovering the reality of life lived in a relationship with God, that includes knowing who we are, where we came from, and where we are going, so enormously outweigh the cost of belonging to Jesus in an alien world, that it is foolish to turn our backs on this wonderful discovery. What we are talking about are matters of great urgency. They are issues of life and death which have to do with discovering the fullness of life that we have here and not allowing it to be frittered away and wasted. It has also to do with the vital issues of where we spend eternity. God allows people to go to hell because they choose to go there, as they reject the forgiveness and the love of God. Jesus talked not only of a real hell but also of the reality of heaven—eternity spent with him. None of us know when we will die and have to face his judgement, therefore it is important that we sort these issues out with God now.

When Jesus told the story of the prodigal son he was talking about a father who was looking and longing for men and women to come back into a relationship with him. In that story he explains why it is that every one of us is separated from God. Nobody can be born a Christian. All of us are born with sin in our hearts, and therefore the principles of greed and selfishness are at work in us right from the very beginning.

In this story Jesus describes the whole nature of sin in very simple terms. He says that a son went to his father and said to him: 'Give me what is mine.' In other words, there are two main elements that are at work in every human being. The first is a desire for independence.

There are many of us who believe in God and who are prepared to go to church and to pay lip service to him, but we don't actually want God to be involved in the important issues of our life. When it actually comes to relationships, money, the future, our household, we want to be independent of God. It may be because our prejudice tells us that God will spoil our lives or it may be that we are afraid he might ask us to do things we don't want to do.

Either way we all want to be independent. It is that independent spirit within mankind that is the very essence of sin. God never intended, of course, for us to be robots or puppets in his hand—he gave us a mind in order to reason—but his intention was that freedom only comes through submission to him.

The other characteristic of sin is selfishness summarized by: 'I want this for me.' If we examine our lives closely enough, all of us will have to admit that at the centre of it all is a desire for ourselves. There obviously are good motivations and loving things that we all do, but ultimately every human being is self-centred. And here Jesus says is the root cause of the problem and we will never come to the solution if we don't admit to the cause. John said, 'If we say we have no sin, we deceive ourselves, and the truth is not in us' (1 John 1:8).

Jesus was saying that the consequence of the sinfulness of human nature is a breakdown of relationship. That is why large numbers of people believe in God but few people know God. Many, of course, are confused and don't even know whether God exists or not, which is not very surprising because they have never met him. The simple truth is that the reason we don't know God is because there is a breakdown in our relationship with him caused by our sin.

Jesus said that sin would cause not only separation but frustration. The young man who disappeared with the money very soon found that it ran out and he ended up on a pig farm. One of the characteristics of human experience is frustration. Everything that is meant to satisfy seems to do so only for a moment and then we want more. This is true of every material and sensual pleasure in life.

And the answer to the problem of our separation from God is in the death and resurrection of Jesus Christ. The cross shows us the justice of God—that sin has to be dealt with. The cross also shows us the incredible love of God, that God was prepared to pay the price for each of us.

It is quite impossible for man to get right with God purely through going to church. Going to church makes you a church-goer, it doesn't in any way change your relationship. How can it?

It is quite impossible to restore your relationship with God by trying to be good. The more we try to be good the more we realize that we can't do it because there is something at work in us preventing us from being what we know we ought to be. If all Jesus did was to come and tell us how to live then all he has achieved is to increase our guilt and our sense of condemnation.

It is also impossible to get right with God purely by believing in him. The Bible tells us that the devils believe and they are certainly not Christians!

There is a story told, which I am sure is fictional, about a lady who had to go to court for quite a serious offence. When she arrived in the court room she recognized the judge because he lived in the same street. This was a tremendous relief to her as she assumed she would get off very lightly. So when she caught his eye she winked at him, but he didn't seem to be terribly amused! At the end of the case the judge summed up and she was found guilty by the jury. He fined her a very large sum of money which in fact he knew she couldn't pay. She was horrified and felt badly let down. As she walked down the street afterwards she saw the judge coming out of the side door. He was dressed in a suit—having taken off his wig and his robes. She wanted to avoid him, but he came straight up to her. She was very angry, but he said to her: 'I am sorry for what happened today. But you see you were guilty and I am a judge. Because you committed a serious crime you had to pay for that crime. Now you know that the penalty has been paid you know that you can be free of guilt. But,' he said, 'I know that there is no way you can afford that sum of money.' He took out his cheque book and wrote out a cheque for the full amount. Then he said: 'As a judge I found you guilty and I fined you. As a friend I'll pay the fine.'

God, as judge of this universe, is utterly just. If he were to condone and forgive sin without any judgement on it he himself, by accepting evil, would be evil. But because God is holy, sin has to be dealt with. As a judge he finds every one of us guilty. But as a friend, as a lover, he pays the price! That is the amazing message of the cross—Jesus paid for our forgiveness. What does it mean? It means that as far as God is concerned every one of us has the opportunity to be completely forgiven for everything we have ever done wrong. And when there is forgiveness there is automatically a restoration of relationship. It is immediate and it is complete—even though it is followed by a process of change.

But each of us has to choose whether we want to receive and accept that forgiveness. As we receive it our relationship with God is restored and we can know him, but part of receiving that forgiveness is also a commitment of our lives to him. It means entering into his kingdom. The doorway to that kingdom is forgiveness.

When we receive the forgiveness that God has given us through Christ and make it our own that is the first step to being a child of God. But there are two sides to the coin. One side deals with the problem of sin. The other is to give us the gift of his Spirit. If we were just to have our sins forgiven and then God sent us back into this world to try our best to be what he wants us to be, he would be committing us to failure. Yet here is the remarkable thing—God gives us a new nature and he gives us the gift of his Holy Spirit.

The person of the Holy Spirit comes to live in us to enable us to be what we are meant to be. He no longer gives us a list of commandments and says, 'Try to keep those.' He actually comes to live within us and enables us to live out his purposes and his ways. The Holy Spirit is given to us as a gift to enable us to be what we are meant to be. He gives us the power to express the very life of Jesus in our lives.

In the story that Jesus told of the prodigal son the

young man went through different steps in order to discover his relationship with the father. Firstly, he realized that he was in a mess. That is the first step for each one of us. We need to have a sense of our own failure and a real desire to be right with God. Secondly, he repented. Repentance is a very simple word meaning change of mind leading to a change of direction. He decided that he was going to get away from his pigsty and go back to his father. His attitude was not of self-righteousness but of knowing that he was wrong and that he needed to say sorry. That is the second step for each of us. Thirdly, he returned. He got up and went home. It is a very simple thing to become a Christian. Every one of us just needs to come and in prayer give ourselves to God receiving his forgiveness and offering ourselves to him.

The next thing that happened was that he was received by his father. His father accepted him and welcomed him with open arms. This was followed by gifts. When we come in prayer and give ourselves to God in this way he receives us with open arms and immediately welcomes us.

Then he wants to give us a gift. It is the gift of the Holy Spirit. When you come to Christ the Holy Spirit is already at work in your life. He is the one who draws you to God. He is the one who helps you to understand about Jesus. Immediately you give your life to Christ, the Holy Spirit begins to work in a new way in your life. But as well as that we need to be 'immersed' or 'baptized' in the Holy Spirit. Jesus said that all we have to do is ask (Luke 11). He said that if we asked we would receive. Many people have difficulty receiving because they are expecting some particular experience. When that experience doesn't happen they assume God didn't answer their prayer. If you ask for the Holy Spirit you will receive the Holy Spirit. The fruit and experience of that will come when you begin to thank him for what you have received. Many people, including myself, have found it a tremendous help to have somebody actually pray with them in this regard. It is a very simple thing to ask another Christian to lay hands on you and pray for you to receive the Holy Spirit in all his power and fullness.

One other aspect that is important. In the Acts of the Apostles when they asked Peter what they needed to do, one of the things that he told them was to be baptized. Baptism in water is part of the Christian initiation.

Enjoying the family

Many people have assumed that going to church and being a Christian are synonymous. Of course, being a Christian has to do firstly with our relationship with God. Going to church is a way of meeting with other Christians and enjoying corporate worship. The important thing for every child of God is to be able to enjoy fellowship and a relationship with other members of the same family. Therefore it is vitally important, if we are to grow and develop in our relationship with Christ, that we meet together with other believers. This may be in a small group or in a large fellowship, or preferably both. But it is important that each of us gets linked in to other believers with whom we can share our lives, from whom we can receive encouragement and strength, and to whom we can give the gifts and talents that God has given to us.

Rise Up and Build

by Nick Cuthbert

How near are we to a revival in Britain today?

Can God's people move on without restoration?

What has been achieved so far by the renewal movement?

The church in Britain has entered an era that is both exciting and challenging. Christians in 'house churches' and in the traditional denominations have come into new experiences of great personal blessing.

But what are we *building?*

Nick Cuthbert brings a word of encouragement and a word of warning. He calls on churches that are weary through failure—and those trapped by yesterday's blessings—to listen to what the Spirit is saying to the churches . . . and then obey.

If we want the church to be an effective force in our land, let's respond to God's call today.

Nick Cuthbert is a founder of the Jesus Centre in Birmingham. He is fully engaged in an evangelistic and teaching ministry.

k Kingsway Publications

The Father Heart of God

by Floyd McClung

What is God like?

Has he got time for twentieth-century men and women?

Does he really care?

In his work with *Youth with a Mission*, Floyd McClung has met many who suffer from deep emotional hurts and fears.

Time and again it has been the discovery of God as Father—perfect and reliable, unlike any human parent—that has brought healing and liberty.

This book is for you . . .

. . . if you find it hard to accept God as a loving father,
or
. . . if you know God's love but would like to share his blessing with others more effectively.

Kingsway Publications

God Wants You Whole

The Way to Healing, Health and Wholeness

by Selwyn Hughes

If God is always willing to heal, why do people remain ill—even when they have faith for healing?

How can we all live more healthy lives, day by day?

With openness and honesty, Selwyn Hughes faces squarely the issues of health and healing that concern every one of us. He examines the most common causes of ill health and the reasons we fail to receive God's healing grace. Here we see how our Creator has lovingly provided all we need for wholeness of living, if only we set ourselves to live in accordance with his will.

Above all, this book shows that even when healing eludes us and our condition is not remedied quickly, we can still rest secure in the knowledge that our heavenly Father is committed to our good—in spirit, mind, emotions, and body.

Also by Selwyn Hughes in Kingsway paperback:
A friend in Need; How to Live the Christian Life; The Christian Counsellor's Pocket Guide; Everyday Reflections; A New Heart; Marriage as God Intended.

Kingsway Publications